TO Alina

The Time of Your Life

With very Best Wishes

Trisha Scott

The Time of Your Life

While You're ... brushing your teeth, texting, sleeping, working, supermarket shopping, having sex ... what else is happening around you, and around the world, for the same 30 seconds, 2 minutes, 8 hours – and more?

I've brought together over 100 activities that cover different time periods, and which give you a snapshot of the wider view of your life.

Illustrated with captioned pictures, quotes, cartoons and factoids, it's a fun and entertaining slant on your life and your world.

Suitable for age 16 years and over

The Time of Your Life

Trisha Scott

Edited by
Rosemary Scott

©2023
The Conrad Press

The Time of Your Life
Published by The Conrad Press in the United Kingdom
2023

Tel: +44(0)1227 472 874
www.theconradpress.com
info@theconradpress.com

ISBN 978-1-911546-21-4

Book cover design by:
Charlotte Mouncey, www.bookstyle.co.uk

Book design and formatting by: Trisha Scott,
www.trishascott.net

The Conrad Press logo was designed by Maria Priestley.

Printed and bound in Great Britain by Clays Ltd, St Ives
plc.

Contents

With huge thanks to those who have made this book possible –
James Essinger, Charlotte Mouncey and Royston Robertson.
And with special thanks to my lovely sister, Rosemary Scott, for
her wonderful help with captioning pictures and editing
The Time of Your Life.

9

The Material

This book is not intended as an infallible reference book. It's more 'food for thought'. The information is from the results of research and surveys and, where they haven't been available, I've taken an average from forums and Internet sites. The material is current or, where necessary, figures are from 'normal' pre-pandemic life.

I've omitted some of the 'abouts' and 'approximately's' and 'average's' for easy-reading. I've included some references and calculations, as space allows.

Of course, you can relate any of what's happening in the different sections to other of your activities for the same 5 minutes, 2 hours, one week, etc., for which I've included a 'Time Index'.

Copyright

I've made every effort to ensure that the material in this book does not infringe anyone's copyright. The clipart I've used was in the public domain at the time of writing. If I've slipped up at all and used anything in copyright, please contact The Conrad Press and I will remove the material from the book.

Equally, this book is my copyright. If you like any of my material and want to share it on social media, or if you use my material, including that in the 'Time Index', to compile articles, blogs, etc - you need to say the material is from this book.

You can't use the cartoons of Royston Robertson, or the captioned pictures and clipart images that are the design of 'Scott', on the Internet, including on personal sites, without permission, and they are not for public domain use. Please contact The Conrad Press for permission to use them.

I hope you enjoy all of them, and I hope you enjoy my book.

> "To laugh often and much; to win the respect of intelligent people and the affection of children; to earn the appreciation of honest critics and to endure the betrayal of false friends; to appreciate beauty; to find the best in others; to leave the world a bit better whether by a healthy child, a garden patch or a redeemed social condition; to know even one life has breathed easier because you have lived. This is to have succeeded."
> *Ralph Waldo Emerson*

A Matter of Time

Introduction

"One day we'll look back at this and laugh … "

Welcome to …
The Time of Your Life

This is a journey that might be an interesting time-filler, or it might leave you wondering how you spend your time.
For example - what else is happening while you're … eating, working, texting, shopping? I've given you a snapshot in this book. It may take your mind on a bit of a whirl – and you might end up questioning the *value* of how you're spending the time of your life.

That 'value' is individual – whether it's financial security, marriage, raising a family, career achievement, friendships, fitness or education – and it changes with age and circumstances. But the value of anything is the amount of life you choose to exchange for it. I hope this book illustrates that you have choices about what to do with your time and what to do with your life.

> **"You will never 'find' time for anything. If you want time, you must make it."** *Charles Bruxton*

After reading this book, if you think 'Yep – it's about time I wrote that novel, learnt to sail, booked that trip to Hawaii …' or 'I'm not where I want to be' - I've also given you some 'Sickie Excuses' to try to grab some time off work. (Good luck with your boss believing those!)

> **"To dare is to lose one's footing momentarily. Not to dare is to lose oneself."** *Soren Kierkegaard*

There are, of course, some things you can never do in your lifetime. You'll never find a right-handed polar bear. They're all left-handed. In Quitman, Georgia, USA, you'll never know why a chicken crossed the road – it's illegal for them to do so. You'll never be able to see 221B Baker Street, London. It was the home of Sherlock Holmes and his companion, Dr Watson, but it doesn't exist. And you can't weigh the earth. We only have an estimate that it's 6,585,600,000,000,000,000,000 tons. You also can't find all the gold in the world. There are about 20 million tons of it in the world's oceans, diluted 1 part to 83 million parts of water.

The Measure of Time:
The Incas measured time based on how long it took to boil a potato.

The longest period of time is Para - 311,040,000,000 years - about 70,000 times the age of the Earth.

Planck time is the shortest meaningful interval of time (10^{-50} secs).

The world record for the shortest measured period of time is one quintillionth of one second (12 attoseconds).

And in terms of Earth events, our 70 years of life is only a blink. The whole of human history is just a dot in the chart below.

Earth Events - Years

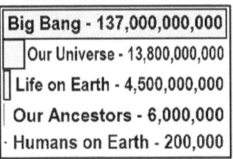

Big Bang - 137,000,000,000

Our Universe - 13,800,000,000

Life on Earth - 4,500,000,000

Our Ancestors - 6,000,000

· Humans on Earth - 200,000

The dot for 'Humans on Earth' should be
three times smaller. It's larger to make it visible.

"The whole life of man is but a point in time; let us enjoy it."
Plutarch

But each of the 2,207,520,000 seconds of our 70 years on Earth is important to us and to others. And how we use that time is precious.

The clock is ticking - there's 86,400 seconds of today that will never come again.

And happiness is by choice ... not by chance.

13

Body Changes

> **"Life is a whim of several billion cells to be you for a while."**
> *Groucho Marx*

Between birth and 70 years old, the following are the number of times that parts of our body are replaced. Our body is not static.

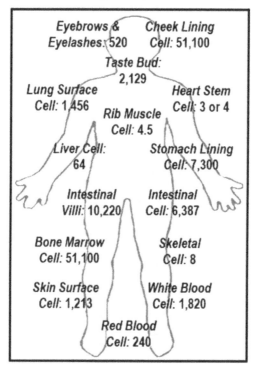

Eyebrows & Eyelashes: 520
Cheek Lining Cell: 51,100
Taste Bud: 2,129
Lung Surface Cell: 1,456
Heart Stem Cell: 3 or 4
Rib Muscle Cell: 4.5
Liver Cell: 64
Stomach Lining Cell: 7,300
Intestinal Villi: 10,220
Intestinal Cell: 6,387
Bone Marrow Cell: 51,100
Skeletal Cell: 8
Skin Surface Cell: 1,213
White Blood Cell: 1,820
Red Blood Cell: 240

Average Time Frame of Cell Replacement

Eyebrows & Eyelashes:7 weeks; Cheek Lining Cell:12 hrs; Taste Buds:12 days; Stomach Lining Cell:3.5 days; Rib Muscle Cell:15.1 years; Liver Cell:400 days; Lung Surface Cells:2.5 weeks; Intestinal Villi Cells:2.5 days; Intestinal Cells:4 days; Skeletal Cell:8.5 years; Skin Surface Layer Cell:3 weeks; Bone Marrow Cell:12 hours; White Blood Cells:2 weeks; Red Blood Cell:3.5 months.
Of our 100 trillion body cells, 24 billion are replaced each day: 613,200 billion from birth to 70 years.

> **"We turn not older with years, but newer every day."** *Emily Dickinson*

In Your Own Time

Your Body

"It doesn't bother me that she's fallen asleep – it's what she's dreaming about that bugs me …"

In Your Own Time
Your Body

You blink an average of 16 times a minute – just under every 4 seconds, making 17,280 blinks in an 18-hour day and 6,307,200 a year.

960 stars have been born in the Universe

It's estimated there are about 50 billion galaxies in the Universe and, assuming they're like our Milky Way Galaxy, there are about 150 billion stars born a year in the Universe. That's about 400 million stars born each day, 4,800 a second; and a star born every 0.0002 seconds (every 2/10,000 of a second) (University of Calgary). So, with an average blink of 200 milliseconds (0.2 seconds) there are 960 stars created in the universe for each blink.

200 photographic flashes could have taken place

... assuming an average blink of 200 milliseconds. 1 millisecond is how long the light lasts for a photo flash. Being that quick, it's a wonder the photo always catches us blinking ...

20 million bits of data have been transferred on the Internet

1 million bits of data are transferred each second on the Internet (1 Mbps). The average download rate (2022) for the UK is 72.06 Mbps, and the USA – 119.03 Mbps. Taking an average of these rates – about 100 Mbps (95.5) - 20 Megabits have been transferred in the time of a blink. That's 20 million bits of data.

The Wi-Fi went down on the train. She clung to the wine list, losing the will to live ...

16

"I adore her."
"I adore him, but if he steps on my toes again, that may change."

You've sussed out how someone's feeling

It takes the human brain 0.2 seconds to recognise emotion in facial expressions – as long as it takes to blink.

Michael Flatley has tapped 7 times with his fantastic flying feet

He can do 35 taps a second – recorded in 1998 for the Guinness World Record.

800,000 emails have been sent worldwide

Each second, 4 million emails are sent worldwide by 4.3 billion email users –50% of the world's population.

Sean tried to copy Riverdance

"It's my back ... my back ... I can't move."

And by the time you next blink: 16 million emails have been sent, and 68 Big Macs have been sold in America

McDonald's sell 17 Big Macs every second in the USA and, with blinks being about 4 seconds apart, they sell 68 burgers in the interval between one blink and the next.

And by the time you next blink after that: there's an earthquake somewhere in the world

The estimate is that every 11 seconds – about every third blink - there's an earthquake in the world. There are about 3 million a year, of which about 10,000 are in Southern California. Most are weak and not recorded, but about 20,000 a year – about 50 a day – are recorded.

And in the time of that blink: The shock waves from an earthquake have travelled 1.6 km/1 mile

The shock waves forming an earthquake can travel at 8 km a second/5 miles a second which, in the 0.2 seconds of a blink, is 1.6 km/1 mile.

> If you have one eye on yesterday, and one eye on tomorrow, you're going to be cockeyed today.

Face-focusing is touching your face. It's an average 2 seconds each time we touch our face. We do so 2 to 5 times a minute.

Face - the Facts:

Each hour, we touch -
- Our nose or mouth 3.6 times
- Common objects 3.3 times

Each day, we touch -
- Our face 2,000-3,000 times
- Smartphones 2,617 times

So, we see our phones as part of us.

OMG! I've lost my phone!

Why do we touch our face?

Thinking, surprise, relief, discomfort, uncertainty, lying, boredom, irritation, flirting, anxiety, correcting our self, to stop saying/hearing/seeing something, scratching an itch, and to know 'I'm here – therefore I am'.

You feel the touch at 270 kph/167.7 mph

We have more touch receptors in our fingers and face – upper lip, cheek, nose and forehead - than other parts of our body. Those on our upper lip are nine times more sensitive than on our leg. Touch neurons travel to the brain at about 75 m/246 ft per second – the equivalent of 270 kph/167.7 mph.

And if you're focusing on Facebook, you're in touch with 228 countries

In numerology, 228 represents: companionship, creative self-expression, optimism, business, teamwork, social interaction, inspiration, relationships, coexistence and tolerance.

It was wise he didn't see her Facebook comments, so she downloaded them to disc and wore it as jewellery.

WHILE YOU'RE ... TAKING A BREATH – IT'S A DREAM

3.33 : seconds

Adults take 12 to 24 breaths a minute – an average of 18. So one breath is 3.33 seconds. And most of our dreams last just 2 or 3 seconds.

So, you can breathe in your good dreams and breathe out your bad ones...

Your mind creates your world

"Just want to wish you sweet dreams, Sweetie."
"Oh no you don't! That's how we got six kids!"

...20,000 a day - the number of breaths you'll take

"Once you make a decision, the universe conspires to make it happen."
Ralph Waldo Emerson

Dream Facts

We have about 1,460 dreams a year. They last from 3 seconds up to 45 minutes, but our brain can make them seem longer.

We dream 1 to 2 hours a night – between 4 and 7 dreams, in REM sleep (National Institute of Neurological Disorders and Stroke). If woken from this REM sleep, we go back into it when we go back to sleep.

Introverts remember dreams better than extroverts (Newsweek).

Men and women have similar bad dreams – 3 out of 4 of each have had the 'falling' dream; and the most common nightmare is being chased.

Life isn't measured by the number of breaths we take – but the moments that take our breath away.

WHILE YOU'RE ... SNEEZING — PUT YOUR HAND AGAINST YOUR MOUTH. THAT'S THE FORCE AN EAGLE HITS ITS PREY - 160 KM/H/100 MPH.

1-5 : seconds

Sneezes: When you sneeze, your body effectively 'stops functioning' – including your heart. It's impossible to sneeze with your eyes open.

Eagles: To catch prey, they combine their diving ability with their acute sight ('eagle's eye'). They can see up to 2.4 km/1.5 miles away.

Bless You!

WHILE YOU'RE ... YAWNING

The average yawn lasts 6 seconds.

6 : seconds

55% of people yawn within 5 minutes of seeing someone else yawn. Reading about yawning makes most people yawn ... like you're doing now?!

Yawning is the body's way of saying there's 15% battery left.

It's your 6 second pause

A yawn lasts as long as the time it takes you to bite your lip or pinch yourself to think straight when you're about to blow a fuse. If you do something different for 6 seconds, then your brain gets back in sync. The reasoning part of the brain (the cortical thinking part) catches up in the 6 seconds, and you become calmer.

> **"To change one's life: start immediately. Do it flamboyantly. No exceptions."** *William James*

 **By half way through the yawn, a cheetah in the grasslands of Tanzania, has accelerated to 99.77 km/h/62 mph**

A cheetah can reach 99.77 km/h/62 mph in 3 seconds from standing. Its top speed is 112.65 km/h/70 mph – matching the highest speed limit on British motorways. High speed car chases of 'Follow that car' were most popular in the 1970s movies.

 Half of those waiting for a website to load give up on it before you finish yawning

53% of us abandon a website if it doesn't load in 3 seconds; 4 out of 5 of us won't retry.

The bite of chocolate you popped in your mouth just before you yawned is about to hit your stomach

Chewed food takes 7 seconds to reach the stomach.

And in North Carolina's Green Swamp, Venus Flytraps have opened their 'mouths' and slammed them shut on 12 insects

The Venus Flytrap takes under half a second to slam shut on an insect.

> About 600 species of plants are carnivorous. Most eat insects but some eat frogs, birds and even small monkeys.

> Please keep talking. I always yawn when I'm interested.

And out there in the Universe a new star is born from a supernova

A supernova is the most energetic single event in the Universe. Material is exploded into space at about 10,000 kilometres per second/6,213.7 miles per second – which is 60,000 km/37,282.27 miles by the end of your yawn. The expanding shockwaves can trigger the formation of new stars.

Swinging on a star

21

WHILE YOU'RE ... HOLDING YOUR BREATH

1 : minute

The average time we can hold our breath is one minute.

In the Greenland Strait, a blue whale is shooting water 15 metres/50 feet high through its blow hole – four times

The blue whale spouts 1 to 4 times a minute at rest, and 5 to 12 times a minute after a deep dive. The single-stream gusher lasts a few seconds and rises up to 15 m/50 ft above the water. It can be heard 2 km/1.2 miles away. With a lung capacity of 5,000 litres/1,100 gallons, the blue whale could inflate up to 2,000 balloons. The average total lung capacity of a man is 6 litres/1.3 gallons of air.

2,640 lightning bolts are hitting the Earth

Lightning strikes the Earth about 44 times a second – 78% of strikes occurring in the tropics (data from NASA earth monitoring satellites). That's 3,801,600 times in 24 hours. Each bolt can contain up to 1 billion volts of electricity and is 5 times hotter than the surface of the sun.

1.6 km/1 mile of traffic has snarled up after a highway accident

The back-up rate is 1.6 km/1 mile every minute.

You breathe oxygen, too? We have so much in common.

ö ö ö ö ö ö ö ö

WHILE YOU'RE ... HICCUPPING

5 : minutes

An attack of the hiccups lasts an average of five minutes. Men get hiccups more often than women.

You have a 2,000 to 1 chance of a thunderstorm

During every one of the five minutes you're hiccupping, there are about 2,000 thunderstorms happening around the world.

HIC!

Serenity is not freedom from the storm, but peace amid the storm.

22

In Australia, two couples got married

With 120,118 marriages registered in one year in Australia, that's 329 marriages per day (365 days) and, assuming a 12-hour day – that's 27 per hour. And that's 2.3 per 5 minutes.

And a golfer has lost his ball forever

The ruling in golf is that you have 5 minutes to search for a 'lost' ball. If you can't find it, it's declared 'lost' and you must take a lost-ball penalty.

WHILE YOU'RE ... FALLING ASLEEP

7 : minutes

On average, an adult falls asleep seven minutes after their head hits the pillow and they've turned off the light.

A whole room of people could be dozing too

There's a systematic lull in conversation every seven minutes. So, if you're feeling dozy at a conference, a lecture or an interview for seven minutes, and then they stop talking ... you could be off to the land of nod – just like that (click) ...

"Where's the cat?"
"Went out, I think."
"A nice quiet night then."

Consciousness: that annoying time between naps.

People who snore always fall asleep first.

 You and your partner could lose 182 calories each - if you kiss the whole time you're falling asleep

... that's 26 calories a minute. 2 out of 3 of us say we're brilliant at kissing!

23

Our moon's travelled 429.5 km/266.91 miles, among 178 moons in our Solar System

Earth has 1 moon, Mars – 2, Jupiter - 67, Saturn - 62, Uranus - 27, Neptune - 14, and Pluto - 5. You can't see them because of their distance, but you're probably gazing in the direction of some other moons than just ours - which travels at 3,683 km/h/2,288 mph. That's 61.36 km/38.13 miles a minute.

And an insomniac is washing the car instead

Same amount of time as falling asleep – a regular level automatic car wash takes 7 minutes.

Sleep Statistics

10%   of couples have considered splitting up over his snoring
14%   of married men hide their teddy bear in the wardrobe or under the bed from visiting family or friends
39%   have trouble falling asleep on a Sunday night
80%   of couples sleep on their partner's side when he/she's away
And ...   men are 4 times more likely than women to sleep naked

---

WHILE YOU'RE ... SNOOZING ON THE ALARM | 30 : minutes

More than 1 in 3 adults hits the 'snooze' button on their alarm clock each day, 3 times before they get up. The alarm's set to repeat after 9 minutes on 'snooze'. So it's a 27 minute snooze and a few minutes to open your eyes.

How to remember your dreams
Snooze alarms are set for 9 minute intervals – stopping you falling back into a deep 'true sleep' (which happens after 10 minutes in your sleep cycle) and stopping you waking up feeling worse than when you first woke up. But you have a lot of early morning REM sleep. So, hitting the snooze button interrupts your dreams and helps you remember them more clearly.
How not to be late
Don't set your clock ahead of real time. If you do, you're 8 times more likely to be late.

He suspected his wife was trying to cure him of ignoring the alarm.

Your eyes will be shut for 30 minutes a day anyway – just from blinking

If you blink at the fastest level of 0.1 seconds each time, for the average 16 times a minute of an 18-hour day, your eyes will be shut 30 minutes a day.

Some people dream of success, while others wake up and work hard at it.

They should invent a Snooze button that hits back.

I do 3 sit-ups every morning. Doesn't sound much, but there's only so many times you can hit the snooze button.

I'm not asleep ... but that doesn't mean I'm awake.

We've come from:
1270: the invention of an accurate mechanical clock - *to ...*
2014: atomic clocks measuring perfect time for 5 billion years

You could be reading a book

The average person reads for 30 minutes daily, with variations in ages. 75 years and over read for 1 hour a day; 15 to 19 year olds – 7 minutes a day. Those who read romantic fiction are good at reading facial clues, are more sensitive, and have better social skills – and women who read 'romance' have 74% more sex than women who don't.

"The publisher will publish your novel – if you make it three times longer or a Christmas cracker joke."

Living involves tearing up one rough draft after another.

We've come from:
600 BC: the oldest written story (the Epic of Gilgamesh) - *to ...*
1474: William Caxton's printing press - *to ...*
2002: Lulu self-publishing company founded – *and ...*
2007: 19th November - the first Kindle

Or driving to Surfers Paradise, on the Gold Coast of Australia, from Coolangatta Airport

From Coolangatta Airport to Surfers Paradise it's a 30-minute drive.

Or enjoying a double-dose of foreplay

A Cosmopolitan magazine survey found that foreplay usually lasts 14 to 17 minutes for the average couple, and a woman takes an average time of 12 minutes to reach orgasm.

Sex

- Sex burns 200 calories in a 30-minute session, including -
  Kissing: 2 calories a minute (more if passionate)
  Groans, squealing and talking dirty: 3-25 calories a minute
  Real orgasm: 27 calories
  Fake orgasm: 160 calories
  Performing fellatio: 30-50 calories (also massages the jaw)
- Erotic sensations travel from skin to brain at 251 kph/156 mph
- Edible underwear: most popular flavour – cherry; least popular flavour – chocolate
- 2 out of 5 women can't enjoy sex unless their partner is intellectually equal; 2 out of 3 men can
- Oral sex – 1 in 3 women swallow

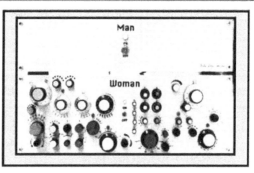

Sexual Arousal – A Guide

26

WHILE YOU'RE ... SLEEPING

8 : hours

Various studies give a range of necessary sleep for an adult from 6.5 to 9 hours a day, to function at your best – average 8 hours.

Sleep is a symptom of caffeine deprivation

You burn about the same number of calories asleep as you would quietly watching TV

A 68kg/150 lb person uses up 61 calories an hour asleep and 68 calories quietly watching TV. For an 8 hour, uninterrupted night's sleep, they burn 488 calories; and with 8 hours of TV instead - 544 calories.

Good natural sleep ...
... lets your brain combine emotional memory. It also diminishes your chances of health problems like diabetes, depression, heart disease and obesity.
Noise from urban living can cause sleep loss – not only for us. 'City' birds wake earlier and rest less than forest ones.

If you're American, half of you are spending the 8 hours with your favourite household member – your dog

Whoever said 'let sleeping dogs lie' didn't sleep with dogs.

A New York Times survey found that 47% of dog owners in America sleep with their dogs. The daily sleep for a dog is 9 hours. 30% of dogs and 8% of cats snore.

27

It's busy in the nearby gardens:

E=mc² but if y=54 and q=12, then E-16/39 + 81³ x 27 divided by blue – I mean 2 – the answer is 42 ... this is doing my head in every night ...

- **Plants are doing maths to save on energy in the dark hours**
- **An owl is catching mice in complete darkness**
- **A mole is digging a 67 m/220 ft tunnel**
- **Cats are seeing six times better than us, savouring the night sights**

Plants use complex mathematical calculations, like human circadian rhythms, to adjust their energy usage. An owl can catch a mouse in the dark - guided only by tiny sounds made by its prey. A mole can dig a tunnel 67.06 to 76.2 m/220 to 250 ft in a night. And, although they can't see in total darkness, cats can see clearly with only one-sixth of the light we need to see, and have better perspective and depth perception than we have. The Ancient Egyptian word for cat was 'mau', which means 'to see'.

Every dog has his day – but nights are reserved for the cats.

And in the gardens of the world:
- **Rabbits in Morocco, pigs in Korea and Guinea pigs in South Africa - are all snoozing**
- **Flamingos in the Bahamas are flying 600 km/373 miles migrating for food**
- **Giant Anteaters in the Guatemalan grassland and Brown Bats in Adirondack Park, Upstate New York are keeping down the insect population with their midnight feasts**

Rabbits, pigs and guinea pigs all get 8 hours' sleep. Flamingos can fly at 50 to 60 km/h/31 to 37 mph and about 600 km/373 miles in one night. The word 'Flamingo' is from the Latin word for 'flame' (flamma). The South American Giant Anteater eats more than 30,000 insects a night, a few thousand at a time from each of the ant nests and termite mounds it visits. It prefers termites to ants, flicking its tongue up to 160 times a minute. It sleeps up to 15 hours a day. The brown bat, common in North America, can eat 500 insects an hour during its night-time feeding – 4,000 a night.

28

It's half a day on Uranus
A day on Uranus is 17 Earth hours. So, your night's sleep and 9 hour working day completes a day on Uranus. It's known as the 'Awakener' in astrology.

You're stirring with sexual twinges
Men have 3 to 5 erections (about one every 1 to 1.5 hours) during REM sleep, each lasting about 30 minutes. Each erection is a combination of blood circulation and testosterone production and a necessary part of REM sleep. Women have similar periodic nocturnal genital arousals during REM sleep. A man's morning erection ('morning glory') is the last in the series of his night-time erections.

You've shrunk 1% by the time you go to bed, and regained the height by the next morning
Spinal discs are mostly water and they're compressed by body weight in standing and walking during the day. Lying down to sleep relieves the pressure and the discs expand between the vertebrae again, so you regain 15 to 25 mm/0.6 to 0.98 inches by morning. You can say that you're taller in the morning than at night. Astronauts can temporarily be up to 75 mm/2 to 3 inches taller in space when released from the force of Earth's gravity.

And, while you're cosying under the duvet, paramedics are trying to save a life in London, Vienna, Cape Town, and Hong Kong ...
... with 24 hour medical cover in most of the world.

> "Dream as if you'll live forever;
> live as if you'll die today." **James Dean**

And the other half of the world is wide awake – working and partying
As always - and when they've gone off to bed - it'll be your turn to 'live the day'.

Taking the Time

Health & Wellbeing

"I know they're orangey but I'm fairly sure you can't count jaffa cakes as one of your five-a-day."

Taking the Time
Health & Wellbeing

WHILE YOU'RE ... PUTTING IN YOUR CONTACT LENSES

10 : seconds

For an accustomed contact lens user and for lenses in both eyes, the average time of putting in the lenses is 10 seconds.

If you see lightning, thunder's closer to you by 3.2 km/2 miles

Sound travels at about 1.6 km/1 mile every 5 seconds (1,223.1 km/h/760 mph). So, after a flash of lightning, for every 5 seconds you count, the thunder is 1.6 km/1 mile away. Because of the high heat produced by lightning, air molecules expand and vibrate so fast that a thunder noise is created.

But somewhere in the world, Cumulonimbus clouds changed to Cumulus ones in 0.17 km/ a tenth of a mile

Cumulonimbus clouds are found in thunderstorms and usually travel about 64.4 km/h/40 mph, and Cumulus – the white, puffy ones like floating cotton wool – are for good weather.

About 20 kg/44 lbs of sunlight has hit Earth

The mass the sun burns into energy every second is over 3.6 billion kg/about 4 million tons. That mass is captured as sunlight at a rate of 2 kg/4.4 lbs a second. In 10 seconds, we have 20 kg/44 lbs of the mass as sunlight.

"Don't move!" she yelled. "I've lost my lens!"

The Sun is 330,330 times larger than the Earth and 109 times bigger in diameter, and about 1,300,000 Earth-size planets could fit into the Sun.

Sunlight can penetrate clean ocean water as deep as 73.15 metres/240 feet.

And in 10 seconds of sunlight, birds, bees, fish and insects have seen parts of the light spectrum that we can't see even with 20:20 vision

Animals seeing ultra-violet light include hummingbirds, bees, goldfish, butterflies and pigeons. Birds see markings in ultra-violet light which attract a mate. But some of these animals (eg birds and bees) lose the ability to see the red-light wavelengths clearly or at all. Some insects have 30,000 lenses (ommatidia) in each eye ball to 'see' movement and muted colour. The dragonfly's brain works so fast that it sees movement in slow motion. Snakes can 'see' the infrared of animal heat with 'vision pits' – a sort of second 'eye' near the nostrils.

And a chameleon is half-way through changing from green to yellow on a banana tree in a Madagascan forest

It can change colour in 20 seconds.

> Definition of a nervous breakdown:
> **A chameleon on a tartan rug.**

🕐 🕐 🕐 🕐 🕐 🕐 🕐 🕐

WHILE YOU'RE ... WASHING YOUR HANDS AFTER USING THE LOO

| **15 : seconds** |

It takes at least 15 seconds for proper hand-washing.

The Café du Trésor in Paris has goldfish in a tank, within the tank of the cistern, in its bathrooms.

Knowing a woman should never go to the bathroom alone, the support group were on-call for all 19 floors of the office block.

32

If you talk to a goldfish, you'll have to repeat what you say 5 times, and it'll still forget

... with its 3 second memory.

The most popular goldfish name: 'Jaws'

On the moon an astronaut, out of his spacesuit, will black out

Without sufficient oxygen, you can go unconscious in 15 seconds – as would happen without a space suit outside the International Space Station or on the moon, which have little or no atmosphere.

A snowy tree cricket, below the window, will tell you the outside temperature

As 'the poor man's thermometer' in July to October – temperature directly affects the rate of activity of this cricket. Count the number of chirps a cricket makes in 15 seconds, then add 40 and you'll be very near the outdoor Fahrenheit temperature.

Beryl decided the weatherman's idea of a 'slightly chilly day' was definitely different to hers.

On the Molokai cliffs in Hawaii, someone's watching for the 'splash' of a stone hitting the sea

The highest in the world, the Molokai cliffs rise over 1,000 m/3,300 feet from the sea. It takes 15 seconds for a stone, thrown off the top, to splash into the sea.

But it would take half that time to land from off the top of the Empire State Building in New York

From falling off the building, it would take 8.81 seconds (using metres per second) or 6.15 seconds (using feet per second) to pass the 102 stories and some of the 6,500 windows and hit the ground (not recommended).

In the Cwmcarn Forest in Wales, UK, a hedgehog's heart is beating 150 times; and, in the Indian Ocean, a blue whale's – about four times

A hedgehog's heart beats about 300 times a minute; a blue whale's heart beats only 9 times a minute, or every 6.7 seconds.

Someone in Japan, Africa, Korea, USA, Germany ... anywhere, has started reading a Harry Potter book

Every 30 seconds, someone in the world starts reading about Harry.

Smile - while you still have teeth.

A red blood cell has travelled round the whole of your body

It takes about 30 seconds for it to circle your entire body.

The sun has pumped over 27 billion kg/30 million tons of material into space

The solar wind carries about 907 million kg/1 million tons of hot plasma of electrically-charged gas particles, at a temperature of about 100,000 Kelvins/99,727° C/179,540.6°F away from the sun every second.

And 1,200 bottles of Scotch whisky have been sent abroad

40 bottles of Scotch whisky are shipped overseas every second, while 20 million casks are maturing in warehouses in Scotland.

The French buy more Scotch per month than they buy Cognac in a year. The most expensive Scotch whisky sold at auction? A bottle of Macallan 'M' 1940 - $631,850 (£489,362).

OLD ORKNEY SPECIAL SCOTCH WHISKY

Your luggage Sir!

STROMNESS DISTILLERY ORKNEY, SCOTLAND

34

2 : minutes

The recommended minimum time is 2 minutes.

"Explain to me again why I need to wear this basque and the black stockings for just a close up shot of the toothpaste."

The most popular colour toothbrush is blue. And you can't pawn your dentures in Las Vegas – it's illegal.

You don't have to brush all your teeth - just the ones you want to keep.

600 million cells in your body are dying and you'll have new ones by this time tomorrow

Of the average 40 trillion cells in your body, 300 billion new cells are replaced every day; 300 million old cells die every minute.

At the New Jersey factory, they've stamped the 'M' on 43,333 'M & M's

About 2.6 million M & M's go to the etching machine an hour. One hundred million individual M & M's® can be manufactured a day; 200 million are eaten daily. 'M &M'' stands for the last names of Forrest Mars, Sr., then candy maker, and his associate, Bruce Murrie.

Your coat of nail varnish should be dry

It's recommended that you wait 2 minutes between coats of nail varnish.

And, in Ireland, someone's just finishing pouring a perfect pint of Guinness

It takes 119 seconds to serve the perfect pint of Guinness. The bubbles in Guinness beer sink to the bottom rather than float to the top as in other beers.

35

WHILE YOU'RE ... HAVING A DENTAL CHECK-UP

5 : minutes

It takes between 2 and 5 minutes for a regular NHS dental check-up in the UK.

I've been to the dentist several times, so I know the drill.

Man: "Do you fancy the favourite in the 3.30 today, Darling?"
Woman: "Well, if it actually finishes the race this time – then yes."

A horse race will be finishing

The longest time a horse race lasts is 10 minutes. On average, flat races last 3 minutes or less, and jump races take between 3.5 and 7 minutes.

While, in a tropical forest of Northern Argentina, a sloth has moved 1.52 m/5 ft

Sloths are the slowest land mammals, moving 0.15 to 0.30 m/0.5 to 1 foot a minute when ambling in trees, and 1.52 m/5 ft a minute on the ground.

Someone's fixing electronic glitches

The average person spends just over 5 minutes a day fixing glitches with electronics.

2 in 5 men buy a new household appliance if one breaks down.

And somebody's a third of the way along Carmel Beach, roller-blading under sunny Californian skies

It takes 10 to 15 minutes to roller-blade along Carmel Beach.

36

An optician's eye test lasts 20 to 30 minutes – averaging 25 minutes (not including choosing glass frames).

"Beauty is in the eye of the beholder, though it may be necessary, from time to time, to give a stupid or misinformed beholder a black eye."
Miss Piggy

"Mildred, I think I need some rose-coloured glasses so all the bad news doesn't look so bad."

Sales Assistant in Optician's: 'Can I help you?'
Customer: 'Yes. Do you sell monocles?'
Sales Assistant: 'Yes, we can find you monocles, Madam.'
Customer: 'Good. Then I'll have one for each eye.'

The Aurora Australis - the Southern Lights – is in full show

The active phase of an aurora display lasts for 15 to 40 minutes and may recur within 2 to 3 hours. So the average time is just over 25 minutes.

And even with 20:20 vision, you can't see what some animals have been experiencing during your eye test

Many species of birds, fish, reptiles and amphibians have better colour vision than we do. Stomatopods (like mantis shrimp) have the most complex colour vision of all animals. Pigeons can see more shades of colour than an advanced computer programme, and millions of colour variations, including near identical shades, over five spectral bands.

We don't see things as they are.
We see things as we are.

WHILE YOU'RE ... SUFFERING FROM A COLD

1 : week

A cold will last about 7 days. There are about 200 known types of cold viruses.

The common cold is the highest cause of sick time off work. You could tell your boss you have 'rhinopharyngitis' or 'acute coryza' (the medical names for a cold).

It's 5 to 1 odds that you'll have a salad; and if you're a Brit, 3 to 1 odds that you'll have fish and chips

Just over 75% of us will have a salad once a week; only 20% will have one daily. 22% of the British public visit a fish and chip shop at least once a week.

Aardvarks Rule OK

If you're poorly in March, sadly you'll miss National Aardvark Week

Every March, the 700 members of the American Association of Aardvark Aficionados celebrate National Aardvark Week.

Over 29 million people are buying a new smartphone

Did you hear – over 1.5 billion people buy smartphones a year?

There are more internet-connected mobile devices than people in the world.

We've come from:
1876: Alexander Graham Bell's telephone - *to ...*
1992: the first smartphone designed by IBM and called 'Simon'

We've spent 3 billion hours in online gaming...

... around the world in a week. Our brain uses 0.1 calories a minute normally. This rises to 1.5 calories a minute during activities like puzzle-solving. A study revealed that chimpanzees solve puzzles for entertainment just as humans do.

38

You'll see 60 coupons, flicking through periodicals

The number in a typical week. After reading the front page of a Sunday newspaper, the next most-read section is the coupon inserts.

You'll take two trips to the library for a 'Star Wars' Fest

In Britain, borrowing up to 4 DVD's for a week from a library – twice - you'll have the 8 feature length Star Wars movies. You can watch one a day during your week's cold, and one on the day after to celebrate your recovery day.

A court heard that a 'Darth Vader' impersonator attacked a founder of Britain's first 'Jedi Church'. The man, wearing a black bin-bag as a cape, apparently used a metal crutch to assault the Jedi church member after leaping over a garden wall. He was drunk. The Judge, sentencing him for probation reports, said that he 'hoped the force is soon with him'.

In Phoenix, Arizona a grapefruit tree has produced nearly 13.1 kg/28.8 lbs of fruit – and your vitamin C

A single grapefruit tree can produce more than 680.4 kg/ 1,500 lbs of fruit a year – 13.1 kg/28.8 lbs a week. Over 20 scientific studies suggest Vitamin C helps fight cold symptoms.

The aspirin you're taking is one of 1.9 billion that people around the world are popping in the week

100 billion aspirin tablets are made and consumed a year - 35,000 metric tonnes/38,580.9 tons. That's 273,972,602.74 aspirins a day, and 3,170.98 a second – and 1,917,808,219.18 the week of your cold.

Children get colds. Men get flu. Women get on.

And you'll drink up to 14 litres of fluid

With having a temperature from a cold or flu, advice is to drink a minimum of eight 250 ml/8.5 fl oz cups of fluid a day. Water's best, and other healthy drinks. A fever makes us sweat and lose body fluids, and our mouth gets dry when we can't breathe through our nose – which also makes us thirsty.

Drink tea and nourish life.
With the first sip - joy. With the second - satisfaction.
With the third - peace. With the fourth - a Danish.

39

WHILE YOU'RE ... WAITING FOR YOUR NHS HOSPITAL TREATMENT (GB)

18 : weeks

Brits have a legal right to start their NHS consultant-led treatment within a maximum of 18 weeks from referral.

Life is a sexually-transmitted, fatal condition.

No, Doctor. I don't want to come in the Sluice Room to check if your beeper is charged up and buzzing.

The Chinese have used 15.5 billion chopsticks

China uses 45 billion chopsticks a year.

24,000 air bags have been stolen in the States

Around 70,000 are stolen each year in the USA.

Don't let people drive you crazy when you know it's within walking distance.

The Czechs have drunk 54 litres/11.8 gallons of beer each

The most beer is drunk by the Czechs - 156 litres/34.3 gallons each annually, followed by Ireland, Germany, Australia, Austria, and Britain.

3,461 new species of insects have been discovered

Scientists find 10,000 new species of insects every year, not including spiders.

And, for every person you meet at the hospital, 942.1 kg/2,077 lbs of concrete has been made somewhere in the world

Nearly 2,721.56 kg/3 tons/6,000 lbs of concrete are produced each year for every person on the planet. That's 7.46 kg/16.4 lbs a day and 52.2 kg/115 lbs a week and 942.1 kg/2,077 lbs for 18 weeks. Concrete usage is twice that of wood, steel, plastic and aluminium combined.

"Be kind, for everyone you meet is fighting a hard battle."

A Legend in Your Own Time

Creating the Image

"Madam, I don't think you've ever looked lovelier!"

A Legend in Your Own Time
Creating the Image

WHILE YOU'RE ... TAKING A SHOWER

10 : minutes

It's an average 5 to 10 minutes for a shower. 70% of men and 57% of women have a daily shower.

Shower Facts
1 in 3 men don't use soap in the shower – they just rinse off.
1 in 4 women hate their partner leaving wet towels on the bed.

A French driver's stuck in traffic
Paris has the worst traffic jams in Europe. Drivers add over 10 minutes to a 30-minute journey losing up to 70 hours a year, the worst being between 8 and 9 am on a Tuesday.

Bob found that, since he'd added the lower jets of water to his cold shower, he'd changed from a tenor to a soprano.

"Well ... great catching up. See you same place, same time – about 8.30 next Tuesday."

Croquet Club (AELTC) at Wimbledon. With the roof closed, you could fit 290 million tennis balls in Centre Court.

Wimbledon's Centre Court roof has been closing
It takes a maximum of 10 minutes for the retractable roof to close over the Centre Court at the All England Lawn Tennis and

Someone's inflating a fitness ball ready for their work-out
It takes 10 minutes to inflate a fitness ball with a foot pump.

And 1 in 4 of us gives our voices a weekly workout fit for the X Factor

1 in 4 of us sings in the shower at least once a week.

☼ ☼ ☼ ☼ ☼ ☼ ☼ ☼

WHILE YOU'RE … SHAVING THAT MANLY STUBBLE

15 : minutes

It's a 15-minute job on work days; 25 minutes on average on the weekend.

Men – Shaving Statistics:
6,585 to 1 – the odds of injuring yourself shaving
5 times a year - on average you cut yourselves shaving
1 in 8,000 – of you go to ER in America injured shaving
Maybe because:
1 in 5 borrow your partner's razor without telling them

Having also devoured his breakfast, the other King of the Jungle's at his watering hole …

… three-quarters through satisfying his thirst. After he's eaten, a lion may drink for up to 20 minutes.

And the other Monarch of the Glen is racing over 16 km/10 miles of his empire

The red deer stag is a classic sight on the Scottish hillsides, and runs at 64.4 km/h /40 mph.

While fun is at hand - 540,000 Lego bricks have been made

It takes one minute to make 36,000 Lego bricks, 2.16 million an hour and about 19 million a year. There are about 62 Lego bricks for every person on Earth.

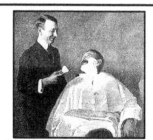

"And our Buy One Get One Free offer is half your moustache off now and the other half off in a week for free."

43

WHILE YOU'RE ... SHAVING YOUR LEGS

15 : minutes

Women shaving both legs from ankle to thigh with a razor and cream – average 15 minutes. 11% of women do so daily.

Dear Shaving Commercials: Please stop shaving hairless legs. If you want to impress us, please shave a gorilla.

Your 15 minute phone chat with a friend could be longer than 7 Twitter posts

We speak 120 to 150 words a minute – averaging 135 words a minute. The 2,025 words in 15 minutes is more than 7 times the 280 word limit of a Twitter post. And your language is one of the 5,000 used worldwide.

Everybody laughs in the same language.

You're missing a quarter of your aerobics class

Aerobics classes last about an hour. 17% of people don't 'survive' an exercise class and walk out of it.

And your pet pig is exercising for 3.2 km/2 miles

Pigs can cover 1.6 km/1 mile in 7.5 minutes when running at top speed.

"Never wrestle with pigs. You both get dirty and the pig likes it."
George Bernard Shaw

Naming a pig 'Napoleon' is against the law in France.

44

WHILE YOU'RE ... GETTING READY TO FACE THE WORLD

15 : minutes

It's the same 15 minutes that it takes a man to get dressed - that it takes a woman to put on her make-up

Men take 10 to 15 minutes to get dressed on a work day; and women take 15 minutes to put on their make-up on a weekday morning.

Statistics
3 out of 4 men buy their own clothes;
1 out of 4 men did in 1975
For 1 in 3 women, make-up is the most important thing of the day
2 out of 5 women use their rear-view mirror for make-up, driving to work
93% of women say make-up is necessary for a night out
Half of women always wear it at work

ⓒ ⓒ ⓒ ⓒ ⓒ ⓒ ⓒ ⓒ

WHILE YOU'RE ... IN THE BEAUTY SALON

1 : hour

For a professional manicure, it takes an hour to fit acrylics. A bikini wax takes one hour, and the average time for a pedicure is 60 minutes.

Beauty Tips
Want some 'me-time'? *Tell your partner you're going furniture shopping. He won't want to come.*
Want to feel special? *Just put on some perfume.*
Want to love your body? *Show off your legs. A compliment about them is an instant lift.*

Girl No. 1: "I'm having a blonde moment."
Girl No. 2: "Naaah! I don't believe you! I know your real hair colour."

Hair Colour:
11% of men don't know their wife's natural hair colour.

42% of women tell only their best friend their natural colour.

45

Throughout the world, 32 women are getting bigger breasts, and 17 – smaller ones

Each hour, 32 women worldwide have breast implants, and 17 are having a reduction.

Hmmm ... Breasts: OMD's - Objects of Man's Distraction.

Getting the Measure of Bras:

3 out of 4 women wear the wrong size bra.

Dark bras may feel tighter than light ones – it's due to the dying process.

Bra sizes fluctuate throughout the monthly menstrual cycle.

You can do a degree in Bra Studies at the Hong Kong Polytechnic University.

A woman adjusted her 42D bra strap, when looking at her reflection on an escalator. The force of the strap snapping sent the 37-year-old mother crashing down the Moscow store's escalator, injuring 15 people on the way.

Your body's replacing 13.75 billion cells during your manicure or waxing

We have an average of 40 trillion cells in our body. 300 billion of them are replaced daily - 13.75 billion an hour and 3,819,444.44 a second. Your body is continually renewing you for life.

And while you're creating your own style, over 100 women in the USA are copying Marilyn's style in one-hour shows

It was naughty, but she liked to ask him – 'Notice anything different about me?'.

The MM impersonators are hired for bachelor parties, stage shows, family events and business trade shows.

"We are all of us stars, and we deserve to twinkle."
Marilyn Monroe

46

WHILE YOU'RE ... BETWEEN SHAMPOOS

2 : days

The average time to wash your hair is every other day.

Hair Facts

It wasn't until the 1950's that women had weekly hairdresser appointments. In the 1890's, they went a month between salon visits, changing to two-weekly appointments after a New York Times piece said it was OK to do so. *The comb was invented in 8,000 BC.* We keep the same hairdresser for 12 years. *The top reason women change hairstyle is to copy a celebrity.*

"Can you do me an Afro with a heavy fringe."

You'll have lost 80 to 200 strands of ... HAIR

We have about 100,000 hairs on our head, losing between 40 and 100 a day normally. Each follicle can grow about 20 hairs in a person's lifetime. Each hair grows about 12.7 cm/5 inches every year, and the average lifespan of a hair on the head is 3-4 years before it falls out.

You'll look in the mirror 76 times (women) and 38 times (men)

Women look in a mirror an average of 38 times a day; men – 19 times a day. Women are more critical, than admiring, of how they look.

A guy you know is about to call his mum

Men think about calling their mum every other day; women – five times a day.

In Yellowstone National Park, the 'Old Faithful' geyser has erupted 34 times

'Old Faithful' in Yellowstone, Wyoming erupts about 17 times a day.

504,000 websites went live

252,000 are created every 24 hours.

47

In July, you've had a choice – watching the Alpine Horn Festival in Switzerland or the British Lawn Mower Association's

World Championship race in Sussex, England

Both last for two days. In July - hundreds of 4 m/12-foot-long alphorns are played at the Alpine Horn Festival in Switzerland for two days. And the British Lawn Mower Racing Association has its two-day World Championship races each year in Sussex, England.

🔔 🔔 🔔 🔔 🔔 🔔 🔔 🔔

WHILE YOU'RE ... WEARING IN YOUR FAVOURITE JEANS

5 : years

Your coffee's getting ready to brew

There's a direct association between your favourite jeans and coffee. The average time of having jeans for them to become a favourite pair is 5 years - which is the same length of time that, after a coffee seed is planted, it produces the fruit for your mug of coffee.

Brewing Up

- The best time to drink coffee? 2.16 pm. Then - your energy levels are low, your metabolism is less effective, and the caffeine might perk you up.
- To remember the value of Pi (3.1415926) - count the letters in each of the words of 'May I have a large container of coffee?'
- 1 in 3 women would go without their partner for a week than go without their coffee.

Every morning –
a new world is born.
Every day –
a new chance.

48

WHILE YOU'RE ... CHANGING YOUR MAKE-UP STYLE

10 : years

On average, women keep their make-up style for 10 years.

Every girl deserves a boy who won't make her mascara run but will mess up her lipstick.

You're also changing your dog
The average lifespan of a dog is 10 years, and you can choose your next one from 701 breeds.

And changing your vacuum cleaner
A vacuum cleaner lasts, on average, 10 years.

If you're American, you've had the chance to count 64 victims of television coma
In a decade, 64 US soap opera characters have been in a coma in the storylines of the TV series.

And you're being counted too
Most countries carry out a population census every 10 years. In some countries – it's 5 years eg Japan, Australia, Ireland, New Zealand and Canada. The information helps Governments allocate resources.

You've lost two teeth, if you're a smoker
A pack-a-day smoker will lose two teeth every ten years.

It's the end of a solar cycle

A solar cycle, is about 11 years, when there's an increasing, then decreasing, number of sunspots. They're areas of strong magnetic activity and they're darker and cooler parts of the sun's surface (about 2,000°C/3,632°F cooler). If isolated in a night sky, they'd be ten times brighter than the full moon, and they can be 2,500-50,000 km/1,500 to 30,000 miles in size and as wide as the planet Neptune. With the sun rotating on its axis every 30 days, a sunspot will be visible for 15 days and not seen for 15 days.

"... And it's 150 for two hours ... No – in the oven ... OK, we'll run through it one more time slowly step by step ..."

49

60 million people have gazed at the Mona Lisa
Over 6 million people visit the Louvre every year and see the Mona Lisa, although they don't realise they're looking at four versions and seeing only one. X-rays showed there are three more versions under the top one.

"So these three artists walked into a bar," said Lisa.
"And the barman said …"
"Yea – so what did the barman say?" asked Leonardo.
"I'll tell you when you've finished my painting," said Lisa.
"I'll have forgotten the joke by then," said Leonardo.
"I won't," said Lisa. "I'll be thinking about it. It makes me smile."

On an Alaskan glacier, an ice worm has cleared the algae, and it's now dying
Billions of black, blue and white worms, less than 2.5 cm/1 inch long, spend their life continuously feeding on snow algae blown onto glaciers by the Arctic winds. They live up to 10 years.

Icy Facts
Cordova, Alaska holds an annual Ice Worm Festival in February.
About 10% of the world's surface is permanently covered in ice.
The subglacial Antarctic Lake, Vostok, has been buried under ice for 15 to 25 million years, but it still has microbial life in it. DNA from over 3,000 tiny organisms has been found there.

They've just finished painting the Forth Bridge again …
It takes 10 years to paint the 2.41 km/1.5 mile Forth Bridge in East Scotland – and it's estimated that they'll do it again in 25 years' time.

Right lads, job jobbed. See you in 25 years.

… while a nearby Scottish barn owl ate 11,000 rodents
A single barn owl, with a ten year lifespan, can eat 11,000 rodents.

Once Upon a Time
Relationships

"Er, whichever one you like,
I like ..."

Once Upon a Time
Relationships

WHILE YOU'RE ... HAVING A FEMALE SOBBING MOMENT

6 : minutes

A woman cries, on average, for 6 minutes at a time, 64 times a year; men – for 4 minutes at a time, 17 times a year (German Society of Ophthalmology).

"I'm selfish, impatient and a little insecure. I make mistakes, I am out of control and at times hard to handle. But if you can't handle me at my worst, then you sure as hell don't deserve me at my best." *Marilyn Monroe*

The world always looks brighter from behind a smile.

"Either the cat goes, or I go."

You'll also laugh for the same amount of time during the day
A world-wide Gallop Poll reveals that 72% of us smile or laugh every day. Also - we spend 6

minutes a day laughing, even though we're not as happy as 60 years ago – when we spent three times as long laughing (Ocean Village poll).

You don't have to attend every argument you're invited to.

Her new hobby was cross-stitching flowers – Deadly Nightshade, Bloodroot, Poison Hemlock, Black Locust ...

And, instead, you could be heading for a great day out at Portobello Road Market

It takes 6 minutes to walk to Portobello Road in London from Westbourne Park Tube Station.

> She who laughs, lasts.

🕐 🕐 🕐 🕐 🕐 🕐 🕐 🕐

WHILE YOU'RE ... GETTING MARRIED

30 : minutes

The marriage ceremony varies from 5 to 10 minutes for a Justice of the Peace wedding to 15 minutes for 'quick vows'. It lasts an hour if it's a traditional Catholic wedding Mass and 30 minutes if it's a typical church or civil ceremony.

> *One of the most amazing gifts in life is to find someone who knows all your flaws, differences and mistakes, yet still loves everything about you.*

Eloping?

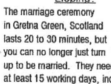

The marriage ceremony in Gretna Green, Scotland lasts 20 to 30 minutes, but you can no longer just turn up to be married. They need at least 15 working days, including for the Registrars to check documents and draw up your marriage schedule. But you can still wear kilts.

If you want Elvis there – you can choose from 50,000 of him ...

... the number of official Elvis impersonators available worldwide at any time.

You'll check your cell phone about 4 times

Millennials check their phone 150 times a day – averaging every 8 minutes of an 18 hour day, and 4 times in 30 minutes. A study found that we open a text message on average 4 minutes after it's been sent – 720 times faster than we open emails - up to 48 hours after they're sent.

---

1 in 2 brides change their Facebook status to 'married' immediately after exchanging vows.

And you can clock up 1.6 km/1 mile of exercise with 30 minutes disco dancing

A disco song averages 120 beats a minute – up to twice our normal adult heart rate (60 to 100 beats a minute). Record producer Tom Moulton extended the original 3 minutes of a disco song to 5 to 7 minutes using remixing, to keep people on the dance floor. So, assuming a dance step for every other beat – 60 steps a minute - and the average disco song is 6 minutes, we take the equivalent of about 360 steps for each disco song for which we hurl ourselves around the floor. Studies estimate that 1.6 km/1mile is roughly equal to 2,000 steps. So, every 5.5 disco songs – every 30 minutes - you've danced 1.6 km/1 mile.

The average honeymoon lasts 8 days.

No. 1 no-no for a groom to take on honeymoon? His laptop.

"I'm guessing that a movie and a curry are not what you're thinking right now."

And 15,000 hours of video are being uploaded on YouTube

Every minute, 500 hours of video are uploaded on YouTube.

What they might not want to remember

The fight and who started it - 1 in 3 DJs has seen one at a wedding
Ex-lovers hovering - 2 out of 3 couples have slept with 2 of their guests
The planning headache – it's the ultimate stress for 1 in 5 grooms
The tipple or 2 the bride had – 2 out of 3 of them will have 2 or 3 or …
The dress didn't fit any more – 1 in 4 brides are pregnant at their wedding

WHILE YOU'RE ... WAITING FOR YOUR DIVORCE

4 : months

A simple undefended divorce should be completed within about 12 to 20 weeks – averaging 16 weeks - assuming there are no complications. You can't get a divorce in the UK until you've been married for one year, although you could apply for a decree of judicial separation or possibly a decree of nullity.

Definition: Divorce – a splitting headache.

A rise in the number filing for divorce in January indicates that the economy is improving.

Where did I go wrong?

Some of your red blood cells are going around your body 345,600 times

They have a 120 day lifespan and circle your body every 30 seconds.

Someday, someone will walk into your life and make you realize why it never worked out with anyone else.

And some of your eyelashes have been renewed twice

An eyelash is renewed every 6 to 8 weeks.

Talking of eyes ...
1 in 6 women, who sneak a look at their ex's Facebook, want to see them really sad and alone.

The Sahara Dessert has grown 4.0 kilometres/2.48 miles

The desert expands about 1 km/0.62 miles a month.

55

A giraffe toddler in Angola has grown 0.1 m/4 inches
Young giraffes can grow 25.4 mm/1 inch a month.

It's half of a day on Venus

A day on Venus (the time it takes to rotate once) lasts 243 Earth days. It's the longest day in the Solar System. Venus also rotates clockwise and 'backwards' to all the other planets that rotate anti-clockwise. So, on Venus the sun rises in the West and, 116.75 days later, sets in the East – opposite to what happens on Earth. Venus may have suffered a huge impact billions of years ago – possibly from a planetoid that flipped it over.

A cat has had 7 kittens
A cat can have between 3 and 7 kittens in a litter every four months.

You cut your chances of having a heart attack by half, by stroking a cat.

My best friend ran away with my husband. How I miss her ...

And you could celebrate 'feeling free' with a bungee jump off the Victoria Falls bridge in Zimbabwe
Adventures, like the Zimbabwe jump, can be booked in advance to be used within 6 months or longer. The Victoria Falls, locally called Mosi-oa-Tunya (the Smoke that Thunders), is the world's largest curtain of falling water and the only waterfall over 1 km/0.62 miles wide. The Zambezi river plummets into a chasm 108 metres/354.33 feet deep, with over 500 million litres/110 million gallons of water a minute going over the falls. Its roar can be heard 40 km/24.86 miles away; the spray and mist rise to 400 m/0.25 miles - visible from 50 km/31 miles away.

Life may not be the party we hoped for, but while we're here we should dance.

WHILE YOU'RE ... A GUY GETTING OVER A BREAK-UP

6 : months

It takes a man up to 6 months to get back on track after a relationship break-up.

You might get your ring back but maybe not your sweatshirt.
Two-thirds of men will have jewellery returned, after a break-up. But 9% of women take their former partner's sweatshirt and don't return it.

Single again – but now with experience.

For 13% of us, a relationship has been ended sitting in a car.

You've walked 2 miles round the room, making your bed

We walk 4 miles a year making the bed. Women make the bed 78% of the time, so a guy goes from making the bed 22% of the time to making his own bed 100% of the time, in a break-up.

A Man's Bedroom Habits ... a Woman's Nightmare

He has 1 set of bed sheets; she likes a choice of 3 - in assorted colours/patterns.

He has no top sheet on the bed; what can she wrap around her?

He leaves clothes lying around; her choice - pick them up or trip over them.

He has no curtains - aahhh! She can't sleep and ... forget sex.

It's time for Dracula to come out of the coffin

Count Dracula has the honour of being the world's top horror character. Dividing the number of Dracula movies (161) since they were first featured in 1931, it's almost two Drac films a year.

BOO!

C. Dracula
1012-1256
1458-
1527-
1703-
1673-

1 in 10 single people go to the movies by themselves once a week.

57

There's been six Ides of the month

There's an 'Ides' in every month, not just March of Caesar fame. The Ides, from the Roman calendar, are on 15th March, May, July and October and on the 13th of every other month. Ides, of roughly mid-month, means to divide.

The US strip industry has earned itself $7.5 billion/£4.25 billion

Americans spend more on strip clubs - $15 billion/£8.5 billion a year - than classical theatres and concerts together.

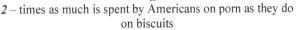

Naked Figures ...

2 – times as much is spent by Americans on porn as they do on biscuits

5 – the number of porn pages for every 'normal' web-page

45% - of men would definitely not want their mother seeing their browsing history

80% - of all pictures on the Internet are of naked women

90% - of movies released in the US are porn films

4.2 million – the number of porn websites in the world (growing daily)

And, if you're in America, you've eaten 23 slices of pizza – a lot of them on a Saturday night with a pepperoni topping

Americans each eat 46 slices (10.43 kg/23 lbs) of pizza every year. Saturday night is the biggest 'pizza-eating' time and the favourite topping is pepperoni (36%).

17% of single men haven't cooked a meal in over a year

FLY SOLO...

"This time, like all times, is a very good one, if we but know what to do with it."
Ralph Waldo Emerson

WHILE YOU'RE ...
EXPECTING A BABY

A full-term pregnancy lasts 40 weeks. Some calculate this as 9.5 or 10 months, but normally we use the traditional 9 months.

More babies are born ...
With a change in barometric pressure, and between 6 am and 1 pm.

You've had 6 months of fun to get your 'bump'

When the sun is riding high
Her love is just platonic.
But, Oh, when the moon is in the sky
And she's had a gin and tonic ...

When are ladies most fertile and sexy? - 11th December
They feel more sexy with Christmas festivities.

Doctor: "Have you ever been bedridden?"
Woman: "Yes, doctor – twice, and once in the back of a car."

Your baby is growing 5,000 million times larger than his/her conception
From fertilization to birth, a baby's weight increases 5,000 million times.

With the baby due in a couple of weeks, Dave began practising sleeping at work and staying awake all night.

Couples take about five and a half months of unprotected intercourse to conceive.

What Happens?

The woman's egg is fertile for 24 to 48 hours after being released.
The man produces 1,000 sperm cells in the space of a heart beat and up to a quarter of a billion when he ejaculates.
It takes 5 to 69 minutes for a sperm to reach and fertilise the egg – at an average of 17.8 cm/7 inches in an hour. *The average ejaculate is about 2.75 ml/0.005 pints. Each sperm contains about 3 billion bases of genetic information – like 750 Mbytes of digital information. If an ejaculate has an average of 180 million sperm cells, that's 135,000 Terabytes of information being transferred in sex. But with only one sperm normally fertilising an egg, 750 Mbytes of data in the sperm combine with the 750 Mbytes of data in the egg.*

There are two solar eclipses

There are at least two solar eclipses a year by a new moon, so you've probably seen one as an expectant mother. The eclipse pattern is repeated every 18 years (the Saros cycle). Total eclipses are rare and usually last 5 minutes or less. The next one to be more than 7 minutes is expected in 2150. The rarer solar eclipse plus planetary transit – the next being Venus – is April 5th 15232. Better get your spot on the nearest hill ready, then ...

Fathers

1 in 3 cries when he sees his baby being born.

The top health-related internet search for men 18 to 35 is 'pregnancy'.

And men in their 40s, entering a mid-life crisis, want to make babies.

Astronauts and Cosmonauts on the International Space Station will sneeze 27,000 times

They can sneeze up to 100 times a day because the dust doesn't settle with the weightlessness - it floats and gets up their noses.

Over 270,000 brains have been at work - giving birth to new product ideas

The U S Patent and Trademark Office granted

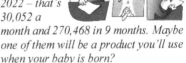

360,625 patents in 2022 – that's 30,052 a month and 270,468 in 9 months. Maybe one of them will be a product you'll use when your baby is born?

The clock was ticking, but he could do it ... a mission through hell and high water. His girl wanted pickles and ice cream and, by golly, she was going to have them.

And cartoonists have finished one episode of 'The Simpsons' and are half way through the next

One episode of the Simpsons takes just over six months to make.

60

WHILE YOU'RE ... WAITING TO GET ENGAGED

1 : year

Expert opinion is that you should wait at least a year before getting engaged to your partner. A recent survey showed the highest number of people (21.57%) waited 1 to 2 years.

The odds of dating a millionaire are 215 to 1.
35% of people using personal ads are married.

"*He loves me, he loves me not ... this guy has some serious commitment issues ...*"

You don't marry the one you could live with; you marry the one you can't live without.

Your future bride may be sporting a whole new hair style
Nearly a quarter of women try a new hair style once a year.

And your clean-shaven fiancé could be a bearded groom
The average beard grows 12.7 cm/5 inches a year.

We'll all be using 6 billion condoms worldwide
Of the 6 to 9 billion condoms sold a year, 70% are bought by men. The average condom user is 18 to 24 years old.

Condoms ... Who Likes What?
In the USA - they prefer the basic sort, and those that use organic materials and lubricants. In Europe – they like textured and shaped varieties. In Brazil – it's menthol and peppermint. The Chinese use the most (the Chinese government buys 1.2 billion condoms a year for family planning) with the British the second highest users, and the USA the sixth.

It was the moment Jeff realised he'd moved the condoms from the glove box to his bedroom in case she said 'yes' ...

The Year of Decision

<u>Getting through it:</u>

Women favour a guy with shared Facebook friends.

On-line: women lie about their looks; men – their income.

It's an average 24 days before you're a 'girlfriend' and 'boyfriend'.

Only 1 in 3 will not have been kissed by 15 years old.

Nearly 1 in 10 takes the full year to fall in love.

Most proposals are on a Thursday.

1 in 3 women are disappointed by the proposal.

Most marry in their early 30's.The average age for brides is 30.8 years, and for grooms it's 32.7 years (2022).

<u>Or breaking up:</u>

It could be one of up to 7 times you'll fall in love before marrying.

It takes half the year to accept the negatives of your lover – or it's over.

After 6 months, the 'sex hormone' cools off and you may not want the same things – from kids to camping holidays.

1 out of 3 women ditch a guy with a bad credit score.

Marrying before 25 years old, or not being stable emotionally, financially and socially, means it may not last.

The texts going between you are part of 8.4 trillion around the world

Globally, 23 billion SMS messages are sent every day and 8.4 trillion text messages are sent each year.

"The very essence of romance is uncertainty."
Oscar Wilde

DIET stands for: *Did I Eat That?*

There's a 2 in 5 chance you'll diet

44% of adults go on a diet at least once a year.

Just as well, because you'll burn three meals at home

Each year, a man or woman burns three home-cooked meals, and 25% of men have started a fire in the kitchen.

The best way to love is to love like you've never been hurt.

62

Ever the perfect housewives, they watched 'Fifty Ways with Pasta' before they got too smashed to care.

WHILE YOU'RE ... GIVING UP ON YOUR MARRIAGE

10 : years

The average British marriage lasts 10 years. The odds of a first marriage lasting 15 years, without separation or divorce, are 1.3 to 1.

So, what would happen if either partner won the lottery? *2 out of 5 men would quit the marriage; 1 out of 10 women would.*

Woman No. 1:
"Aren't you wearing your wedding ring on the wrong finger?"
Woman No. 2:
"Yes – I married the wrong man."

Game Over

Man No. 1:
"What did your wife do before you divorced her?"
Man No. 2:
"A lot of things I didn't know about."

You've had sex twice a week and a total of 1,030 times

The Durex World Sex Survey found we're having sex 103 times a year (1.98 times a week). 22% of men are more likely to refuse sex than their partners are.

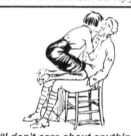

"I don't care about anything else right now," said Susie. *"I've been watching 50 Shades of Grey."*

You think about a new mattress

In 10 years, a mattress doubles in weight with millions of fungi cells, bed bugs, sweat (about 100 litres/175.98 pints/ 22 gallons a year each), and an accumulated 453.6 g/1 lb a year of 6 billion dust mites.

You're taking 11 steps where you used to take 10

We walk 10% faster than 10 years ago.

You're likely to buy a new treadmill

A treadmill has a life-span of about a decade.

You're less likely to buy a coffin

Just over 10 years ago, sales of coffins were at a high – now sales have been dropping annually.

63

"You must see that 'I'll have the bricks and she can have the mortar' is not very helpful?"

When does my marriage licence expire?

Women – objects of affection

Pets – 1 in 10 love them more than they love their partner; 32% - as much as their partner

*A gallon of ice cream – in one sitting within a week of a partner's infidelity

Themselves – 3 out of 4 women want 'me-time' more than they want sex

*('Desserts' is 'Stressed' spelt backwards.)

And, as a woman, you're twice as likely to rob a bank – with a 50% chance that it's one of your Friday list of jobs

Twice as many women are robbing banks today than they did 10 years ago; and nearly 50% of all bank robberies take place on a Friday when shops deposit the week's takings.

To Do List
Friday ~
1 Collect dry cleaning
2 Wash car
3 Rob bank

When life throws you lemons, make orange juice, and leave them wondering how the hell you did that.

Embracing the Moment
Sex

"I appreciate it that you've quit smoking, but eating crisps after sex is just *wrong*."

Embracing the Moment
Sex

German studies are that a woman's orgasm lasts for 1.7 seconds.

You'll have two 'thrills'

An orgasmic contraction is about 0.8 seconds. That makes it about 2 contractions for a woman's orgasm. A man's contractions are the same rate but they have seven times more of them.

Ooh la la!

Laughter is like an orgasm ... nicer if you don't fake it.

Your brain is twinkling like stars

Your brain normally sparks using 100 billion neurons – the same number as there are stars in the Milky Way. But, with orgasm, parts of it are more active – in the areas responsible for learning, memory and social-emotional evaluation (the hippocampus and frontal cortex). The part responsible for emotion and behaviour (the amygdala) is also more active, though that part is less active for men during ejaculation.

A friend confused her Valium with her birth control pills. She has 12 kids but doesn't really care.

900 pairs of shoes are being bought

Globally, 14.5 billion to 19 billion pairs of shoes are bought a year. Averaging, 16.75 billion a year, that's 531.14 a second and 902.94 pairs in the 1.7 seconds of orgasm.

1 in 4 women consistently orgasms during sex

And you might have downed your tipple of wine

There are 5,302,500,000 adults over 18 in the world. In 2022, 23.4 billion litres/41.2 billion pints of wine were drunk worldwide. So you average drinking 4.4 litres/7.7 pints of wine a year. A standard bottle of wine is 0.75 litres/1.3 pints, so you've possibly had a sip or two of your average 5.9 bottles a year per adult worldwide.

66

WHILE YOU'RE ... UNDOING A BRA WITH YOUR TEETH

2 : seconds

It takes 2 seconds to undo a woman's bra with your teeth, and you burn 87 calories.

It's lift-off for 3 planes around the world

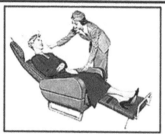

Lady to stewardess: "I can't get up. The cabin pressure on my water bra is pinning me to the seat."

With 38.9 million airline flights worldwide annually (the normal figure, pre-Covid), that's 106,575 a day and 1.23 a second – or between 2 and 3 every two seconds. In those 2 seconds, aircraft engines suck in 2,267.96 kg/ 2.5 tons of air for take-off – about two squash court's worth in volume.

 ### And a whale is sucking in air – 2,000 litres/ 440 gallons worth

When a whale surfaces and breathes, it sucks about 2,000 litres/440 gallons of air within 2 seconds.

🕉 🕉 🕉 🕉 🕉 🕉 🕉 🕉

WHILE YOU'RE ... HAVING AN ORGASM – MEN

12.4 : seconds

German research - a man's orgasm lasts an average of 12.4 seconds and, with orgasmic contractions at 0.8 second intervals, he has about 15 contractions. ●

The population of America is increasing by two people

In the USA, every 8 seconds someone's born, every 12 seconds someone dies, and every 28 seconds an immigrant arrives – so the total population increases by two people every 12 seconds.

Yesss!!!

It's 12.4 seconds of your favourite thing

It takes 116 muscles to climax, and 17 to smile, but men are more willing to climax than smile. Those 12.4 seconds of climax are more important to them.

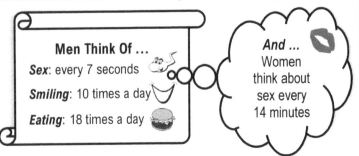

Men Think Of ...

Sex: every 7 seconds

Smiling: 10 times a day

Eating: 18 times a day

And ... Women think about sex every 14 minutes

You can also be saving your soul

A church in Hokksund, Norway, offers salvation in 12 seconds to anyone who reads a two-line prayer out loud from its website. They get the message of 'Congratulations! You have received salvation!'

Facts about Sex

How fast does a man come? 43.5 km/h/27 mph

How many sperm each time? 180-400 million – an average of 280 million (the same as a rabbit, 5.5 times more than a mouse and nearly 30 times less than a pig). In polluted areas, men's sperm count is less than half that of 50 years ago.

What's the average erection? 14 cm/5.5 inches. A smaller soft penis can expand more than a larger soft one but both are about the same size when erect.

And an ice cream van could be playing an appropriate ditty – choose from 'Match of the Day', 'The Stripper' or 'The Entertainer' and, of course, there's a jingle for Mr Softy too

Regulations governing ice-cream vans in GB are that they can be heard for 7 hours between 12 noon and 7pm, with jingles or chimes in 12 second bursts that must be 2 minutes apart.

It's nearly double the time difference between success and failure of the Apollo moon landing

The Apollo 11 lunar module landed on the moon with only 15 second's worth of fuel left.

John practised every day, to perfect his bra-undoing technique ...

The Overhead Dive to the Centre Back

The Squat Behind and Bullseye Target

The Pretend to Hug and Grab It Behind

And someone's nearly rocketed down to Earth

At The Queen Elizabeth Olympic Park, London, the ArcelorMittal Orbit Tower is the World's longest and tallest tunnel slide. It's 114.6 metres/376 feet tall and snakes around the tower five times, ending in a straight 50 metres/164 foot stretch to the ground. Descent speed peaks at 24 kph/15 mph with the ride lasting 30 to 40 seconds.

Right-handed men using their left hand take over twice as long (58 seconds) to remove a bra, and one poor guy took 20 minutes. And there's the sad tale of a man who twisted his finger in a bra strap when he tried to undo a bra, fractured the finger and damaged the ligament. The finger was put into a splint for three weeks after surgery, but was back to bra-undoing fitness in six weeks.

But if you're parked up in America, your car could be stolen while you're – um – occupied

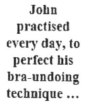

Every 25 seconds, a car is stolen in America, and the top choice is the Honda Accord.

69

WHILE YOU'RE ... HAVING SEXUAL INTERCOURSE

7.3 : minutes

Studies found that sexual intercourse (the time between penetration and ejaculation - not including foreplay or bonding afterwards) averages 7.3 minutes, within a range of 2 to 15 minutes.

Where the fuck did 'Fuck' come from?

One controversial explanation: 'Fornicate Under Command of the King' - from when fire, wars and plague left England under-populated and the King issued the official order.

But the word's been around since the 16th century.

"Wow, Steve. I didn't know we could have so much fun without using Wi-Fi."

Half a million others are having sex

There are about 100 million acts of sexual intercourse worldwide each day. This is 4,166,666.66 an hour, 69,444.45 a minute and 1,157.41 a second – and 506,944.48 in 7.3 minutes. So, you're half-way to being 'one in a million'!

And over 1.3 billion are thinking about it

At any moment, it's estimated that 25% of people are going about their day while thinking about sex. There are 5,302,500,000 adults over 18 in the world. Minus the 100,000,000 having sex, a quarter of the remaining 5,202,500,000, is 1,300,625,000 adults thinking about sex during the day.

Ooo – I fancy a bit of rumpy-pumpy ...

Ooo Yea!! You read my mind ...

Sex appeal – please give generously

Ithyphallophobia

- is the fear of seeing or having an erect penis.

Intimacy means ...

A guy is thrusting an average 90 times (60 to 120) during intercourse, and his testes enlarge 50%.
Most women (85%) are happy with their partner's penis. It's the 9th important factor for them – the 3rd for men.
For both sexes their heart rate rises to 140 beats a minute during orgasm.

More people are tweeting than having sex

There are 500 million tweets a day – 347,222 a minute. In the 7.3 minutes of sexual intercourse, this makes 2,534,720.6 tweets compared to 506,944.48 acts of sex. So tweeting is more popular than sex.

You could have your dinner cooking

A pot of instant rice should be ready in 5 to 10 minutes. It's pre-cooked rice that's been dehydrated -just add boiling water and let it swell.

"Are you tweeting this?"

Number Crunching

Men:

10 seconds – it takes to get a 'hard on' (under 40 years old)
2 in 5 - want sex more often
1 in 3 – lie to have sex

Women:

34 years – the age you feel sexiest
2 out of 3 – are not bothered about having more sex
3 out of 4 – prefer one lifetime sex partner; 25% - up to 100 men
1 in 10 –lie to have sex

Both Sexes:

1 in 50 – claim they've had sex in a plane

71

While the Earth's moving – well actually it's flickering …

… with light flashing round it at 7.5 times a second at the equator. With 438 seconds in 7.3 minutes, that's 3,285 light flashes while you're having sex.

And statistically you should be meeting with someone else

We meet 124,964.08 people a year – making an average of 342.37 a day, 14.3 an hour and 1.8 in the 7.3 minutes of sexual intercourse.

Want a threesome?
Your best bet is Australia. 28% say they've tried it.

While over 13,500 mattresses are being sold in the USA

1 billion mattresses are sold in the States each year – making 1,902.6 a minute and 13,888.9 in 7.3 minutes.

And over $454,000/£365,000 worth of sex toys are being sold worldwide

Global sales of sex toys were $32.7 billion/£26.33 billion in 2022, making $62,214.6/£50,102.7 a minute and $454,166.6/£365,749.5, in 7.3 minutes. As a comparison, that's 90% more than the global sales value of electric toothbrushes. In 2022 those sales were $3.32 billion/£2.67 billion - $3,616.59/£2,912.51 a minute and $46,111.1/£37,134.19 in 7.3 minutes. So, in the 7.3 minutes of sex, about $408,055.5/£328,615.3 more was spent on sex toys than on electric toothbrushes.

More Number Crunching

12.5% - the sex industry has grown since 2008
65% - of US women own a sex toy
70% - of men and women in Italy have used a sex toy
$1 billion – what the US market for vibrators is worth - and the top 3 states for using sex toys are Wyoming, Alaska and North Dakota

---

And you've beaten The Beatles' single 'I Want You'

The Beatles' song is 7 minutes 47 seconds. You beat it by 0.29 seconds.

WHILE YOU'RE ... WAITING AS LONG AS YOU CAN BEFORE SEX

10 : hours

According to one Caribbean cruise line, 58% of passengers can wait only 10 hours before making love. Favoured places are the stateroom and balcony; a lifeboat is the fourth most popular place - the whirlpool bath is the first.

Not one shred of
evidence supports the
notion
that life should be serious

Only 50% of
'Excess' is 'SEX'

Cruise Sex

Is more often and better – the top activity (90%) - beating the pool, nightlife and shopping; and *31%* prefer night sex; *28%* like it any time – day or night

Is more romantic – watching sunsets or stars, taking moonlight strolls and sharing dinner for two

Beats other types of holidays – when only 30% of men prefer sex more than other activities, and 25% of women opt to read instead

 You could have run two marathons and had a cold shower

2 out of 3 runners think about sex while running

According to Verywellfit.com, the average US marathon finishing time is 4.30 hours for men, and 4:56 hours for women.

Your world has spun 16,093 km/10,000 miles
The Earth spins at 1,609.34 km/h/1,000 mph at the Equator.

"Sex is part of nature. I go along with nature." *Marilyn Monroe*

73

It's been a day on Jupiter

A 'Jupiter Day' is the equivalent of 10 Earth hours. The core temperature of the planet is about 24,000 °C/43,000 °F.

And your two time zones are a quarter of a second apart ...

... that's the time zones of the Earth's core and its surface. The Earth's inner core is a moon-size ball of iron, floating in an outer core of molten metal. The inner core rotates in the same direction, as the Earth, but independently of it, and about two-thirds of a second faster than the Earth each day. In 10 hours it spins 0.275 of a second faster than the surface of the Earth. The Earth's core is 6,000 °C/10,832 °F and hotter than the surface of the sun - 5,726.6 °C/10,340 °F. Its geomagnetic field is used as a compass by animals like caribou, sea turtles, whales, birds and fish.

- ❖ I think I could fall madly in bed with you.
- ❖ My sexual preference is often.
- ❖ Don't worry - it only seems kinky the first time.
- ❖ An erection is like the Theory of Relativity – the more you think about it, the harder it gets.
- ❖ The difference between light and hard is that you can sleep with a light on.

🕐 🕐 🕐 🕐 🕐 🕐 🕐 🕐

WHILE YOU'RE ... WORKING THROUGH THE KAMA SUTRA

5 : years

With the average frequency of sexual intercourse (103 times a year, page 63), it would take a typical couple over five years to try every one of the 529 positions described in the Kama Sutra.

... and then they realised they were not on the same page.

"OK. If you really want position 18 instead of 52."

74

You could be one of 55,000 through A & E with imaginative problems

Over 11,000 Americans hurt themselves trying out bizarre sexual positions every year, though in three States, they can't complete the Kama Sutra. By law, a woman can't be on top in sexual activities in Massachusetts; and you must have sex in the missionary position in Florida and North Carolina – and have the shades pulled!

> There was a young lady from Norway
> Who hung by her toes from the doorway.
> She said to her man –
> 'Get off that Divan,
> I think I've discovered one more way!'.

And she can propose in the Leap Year

In the 5 years, you'll have a Leap year with an extra day of February 29th. That is traditionally when a woman can ask a man to marry her.

> ➢ Sex is not the answer. Sex is the question. 'Yes' is the answer.
> ➢ Sex with you is so good that we should celebrate it by having sex.

☺ ☺ ☺ ☺ ☺ ☺ ☺ ☺

WHILE YOU'RE ... IN YOUR LAST MOMENTS AS A VIRGIN

| 17 : years |

According to the Durex Global Sex Survey, people normally lose their virginity at 17 years old.

Virginity is a bubble in the froth of life – one prick and it's gone.

"Darling, fate bought us together."
"You mean – we're the only two with a Facebook status of 'Virgin'?"

75

You can leave your lover when you want

Both as in - getting a driver's licence and motoring out of their life, and emigrating to another country – both of which you can do in the UK when you're 17. Different detailed laws apply to different countries.

Virginity - Who and Where

You've got a 40% chance of it being the person you eventually marry.

Worldwide, 2 in 5 people marry their first love.

Your first sexual intercourse is most likely to have happened in the bedroom.

That's the most common place for intercourse; the car is the second.

The Universe has also evolved

It's expanding at 73 km/45 miles a second. In 17 years it's expanded 38,825,488,373.7km/24,125,040,000 miles.

And you've been on Earth twice as long as 'Beatle Mania'

The Beatles' first gig as the John, Paul, George and Ringo line-up was at the Indra Club in Hamburg on 17th August 1960. The last public performance of the 'Fab Four' was on 30th January 1969 on the roof of the Apple building in London – their first public performance since 29th August 1966. They played publicly for about 8.5 years.

Think highly of yourself, for the world takes you at your own estimate.

All in Good Time

Domestic & Family

"I don't know what he gets up to in there, but it keeps him busy."

All in Good Time
Domestic & Family

To boil a medium, soft-boiled egg takes 3 minutes.

Approach love and cooking with reckless abandon

"We may need a cleaner for the kitchen. When the recipe said heat the egg for 3 minutes, it didn't mention adding water ..."

"An egg is always an adventure; the next one may be different."
Oscar Wilde

Your toast's ready at the same time
It takes 2 to 3 minutes to make a piece of toast using a toaster.

There's been 1,530,000 comments on Facebook
In one minute on Facebook there's: 510,000 comments, 400 new users, 54,000 shared links, 4 million 'Likes', 9.7 million messages sent, 293,000 statuses updated, and 136,000 photos uploaded.

And they're serving eggs Sunny Side Up on Restaurant Row in Manhattan
That's West 46th Street, between 8th and 9th Avenue - 'Restaurant Row' was officially named in 1973. Sunny Side Up eggs take 3 minutes.

78

Averages are: 20 minutes to eat lunch and dinner/tea, and 30 minutes to eat Saturday breakfast.

Lunch & Dinner/Tea: 20 minutes

For 1 in 3 women around you – the most talked about subject is lunch – where and what.

The Joy of Cooking

Americans have eaten 420,000 slices of pizza

 350 slices a second

Home Cooking: where many a man thinks his wife is.

You'll ...
Lose up to 150 calories - *Preparing and serving food is 100 calories an hour; eating a meal burns 50 calories.*
Swallow 295 times – *The average for eating dinner.*
Sit in the same place – *We nearly always do so when we eat at home.*
Have a 50% chance it's a frozen dinner – probably Saturday or Monday – *Half of us always have a frozen dinner in our freezer, and the average person eats 6 TV dinners a month – 20% of the time. A survey found that people dreaded making dinner on a Saturday and a Monday.*
And it's a 1 in 5 chance you'll watch TV – *23% of families watch TV every night during dinner; 23% never do and the rest – occasionally.*

Teatime TV is always fun! You never know if you're going to be the aerial or you're going to eat.

79

Men spend a quarter of the meal chatting; women – three quarters

Men take 5 minutes to talk about their day; women – 15 minutes.

Well, if you hadn't interrupted me telling you about Maisie's new hair colour, I wouldn't have burnt the dinner.

"I like to do all the talking myself. It saves time and prevents arguments."
Oscar Wilde

Talking of which ...

Hippopotomonstrosesquippedaliophobia is the fear of long words.
The top reason we stop listening is when someone's complaining.
3 out of 4 of us want to interrupt when listening to our partner.
The top reason for an argument is we don't listen to what the other's saying – causing some of our 112 rows a year.

My wife says I never listen to her. At least, I think that's what she said.

Men describe their day with 55 words; women with 166

A study showed that both men and women speak about 16,000 words a day, which is 666.67 an hour and 11.11 a minute. Recent research is that women have more Foxp2 (the 'language protein') in their brains which could make them chattier.

I had some words with my wife, and she had some paragraphs with me.

The average time a woman can keep a secret is 32 minutes.

While, far away in a Sumatran forest, a pair of gibbons are chatting just as we are

Siamang gibbons pair for life and make up a song personal to just themselves, lasting 10 to 20 minutes and being one of the most complex of the primate communications. Their patterns of phrases and notes fulfill the criteria of being a song, and scientists Marshall and Marshall said it is 'the finest music uttered by a wild land animal' (1976).

Saturday Breakfast: 30 minutes

*We have a rushed 5 to 10-minute breakfast on a work day,
but indulge in a leisurely weekend breakfast of about 30 minutes.*

It's likely to be in front of the TV and a 50% chance of being cereal

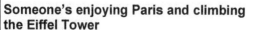

*The most popular place to eat breakfast is
in front of the TV. In a year, you'll eat a bowl of*
cereal about 200 times; and you'll eat 5.9 kg/13 lbs of
it a year.

Someone's enjoying Paris and climbing the Eiffel Tower

*It takes 30 to 40 minutes to climb to the second floor of
the Eiffel Tower – the highest level open to the public.*

And 162 million queries are being searched on Google

Every minute of the day, 5.4 million queries are Googled.

WHILE YOU'RE ...
WALKING THE DOG

30 : minutes

*The average time for walking a dog is 30 minutes. Dog owners are
80% more likely to exercise than non-dog owners, and to do so for
at least 1 hour a week.*

You're taking 3,000 steps

*Studies
estimate that
1,000 steps
equal 10
minutes of
brisk walking – 3,000 steps are
30 minutes walking. That equates
to 2.4 km/1.5 miles - 2,000 steps
equals 1.6 km/1 mile. Climbing a
flight of 10 steps is like 38 steps
on level ground.*

*"And that rain yesterday ... my human
wanted to drag me out in it. And I'm like –
no way. If you want to go - then you go.
I'm staying here on the sofa."*

You've exercised 162,000 muscles

We use 54 muscles every time we step forward.

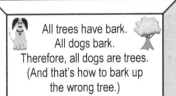

All trees have bark.
All dogs bark.
Therefore, all dogs are trees.
(And that's how to bark up the wrong tree.)

As with humans, so with dogs ...
"Does my bum look big in this dress ... tell me – really. Does it?"

You're gazing at the same moon as are a six-year-old boy in New Delhi, India and a 43-year-old housewife in Perth, Australia ...

... and so many others around the world at night.

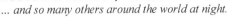

WHILE YOU'RE ... MOWING THE LAWN

| 1 : hour |

Using a regular push mower, the lawn takes an hour.

The grass may be greener on the other side of the fence, but you still have to mow it.

You're moving over 400 litres/88 gallons of fresh air through your lungs and round every part of your body

In a day, adult lungs move about 10,000 litres/2,199.69 gallons of air – 416.67 litres/91.66 gallons an hour and 6.94 litres/1.53 gallons a minute.

Of all hobbies, we spend the most money on gardening.

62% of us who are homeowners have never watered our lawns.

The odds of injuring yourself from mowing the lawn are 3,623 to 1.

"The only difference between a flower and a weed is judgement."
Wayne Dyer

Weeds for Sale

In the Arizona desert, an orb weaver spider has busied away to finish its web by the time you've finished mowing

It takes about an hour for a spider to construct an orb web.

No two spider webs are the same, and spiders react to what they eat. In the 1960's, a study was carried out on the effects of various substances on spiders. When spiders were fed flies that had been injected with caffeine, they spun very 'nervous' webs. When they ate flies injected with LSD, they spun webs with wild, abstract patterns. And when given sedatives, they fell asleep before completing their webs.

In an Illinois forest, a scarlet tanager is eating over 2,000 caterpillars

The scarlet tanager can eat up to 2,100 gypsy-moth caterpillars in one hour.

83

WHILE YOU'RE ... AT THE PTA MEETING

With various lengths of PTA meetings, they average 1.5 hours including after-meeting discussions.

If you can read this, thank a teacher.

Aaah, Shucks!

Teacher: "Now, Jenny – I want all your responses to be oral. What school did you go to?"
Jenny: "Oral."
Teacher: "How old are you?"
Jenny: "Oral."

For Parents' Evening, the maths mistress went for that small, personal detail that set her apart from the other teachers.

In Marrakesh, Dubai, Philadelphia and Toronto – and hospitals around the world - patients are having their appendix out

The appendectomy can be performed in under an hour or can take two hours – averaging 1.5 hours.

Surgeons who play video games cut down mistakes during operations by 37%.

Nurse – I won Level 5 of 'Vampire Monsters' last night, so we could be OK here

355,345,272 litres/78,165,000.06 gallons of water are flowing under Tower Bridge, London

236,896,848 litres/52,110,000.04 gallons of water flow under Tower Bridge an hour.

84

An ostrich egg will be hard-boiled
The biggest egg in the world and the equivalent of about 2 dozen chicken eggs, it takes an hour to soft-boil and 1 to 1.5 hours to hard boil an ostrich egg (the American Ostrich Association). An ostrich egg can make about 11.5 omelettes.

In a study of 200,000 ostriches over a period of 80 years, not one reported a single case where an ostrich buried its head in the sand (or attempted to do so). It's thought that the myth comes from the bird lowering its head when feeding.

Over 3.5 million pairs of socks are being sold
Globally, 21.24 billion pairs of socks are sold each year, which is 2,424,657.5 an hour and 3,636,986.25 in 1.5 hours. Worldwide, about 50% of men use socks daily.

You could be on a Voodoo Tour in New Orleans
The average time for the tours is 1.5 hours.

You can't scare me ...
I have children.

"It's for you! NASA's stumped again!"

Someone's on a hospital couch, donating blood
From the interview to the refreshments afterwards, it takes about 1.5 hours to donate blood. Donating plasma takes about 45 minutes to an hour.

Word got out they were giving wine and chocolates after donating blood.

Nurse: "What type of blood have you got?"
Patient: "Red."

WHILE YOU'RE ... RUNNING A DISHWASHER

2 : hours

Consumer Reports on dishwashers found they have a cycle time range of 80 minutes to 145 minutes. Most of the dishwashers rated were in the 110-125 minutes range, averaging about 2 hours for a full cycle.

Families run a dishwasher an average of 200 times a year.
2 in 5 of couples argue how to load the dishwasher.
70% of us have a dishwasher but don't use it because we don't trust it.

"Oh, look!" she said. *"A clean glass – and I have a full bottle of gin ..."*

The dishwasher's travelled 215,600 km/134,000 miles around the sun. Oh – and so have you

The Earth orbits the sun at 107,800 km/h/67,000 mph. Every second of every day, we're all moving 29.9 km/18.61 miles round the sun.

Doctors are doing hospital ward rounds in Paris, Kuwait City, Oxford ... worldwide

Two hours is an average time for a doctor's ward round. It was recommended at Hôtel-Dieu Hospital in Paris in 1661, and is also now suggested by hospitals in other countries from Kuwait City to Oxford.

"At least we know we've got one examination right today."

PYSCHIATRY DEPT.
ROUND THE BEND

An apple a day ... keeps anyone away, if thrown hard enough.

You could be on the official tour of Buckingham Palace

The State Rooms tour lasts 2 to 2.5 hours. Buckingham Palace has 775 rooms, though not all of them are on the tour.

The Royal Bees

What you won't see, on a tour of Buckingham Palace, are the beehives hidden on an island of wild flowers in the gardens of the Palace. They harvest 160 jars of honey a year, which is enjoyed by the Royal Family.

"Next time," thought Jackson, "someone else can count the bees for the inventory and I'll count the carriages."

...or at a rock concert

Ranging from 1 to 3 hours, the average rock concert is 2 hours.

Jim Morrison, of the Doors, has been immortalised. A recently-discovered prehistoric lizard - Barbaturex morrisoni – has been called 'The Lizard King' – the name that Jim Morrison called himself.

Deaf to the bullshit, blind to the fake shit, It's my life and I'll be damned if I waste it.

WHILE YOU'RE ... DOING THE HOUSEWORK

2-2.6 : hours

WOMEN: 2.6 HOURS A DAY   *MEN: 2.0 HOURS A DAY*

Surveys found that both sexes spend 15 to 30 hours a week doing housework (cooking, gardening, cleaning and laundry). On the days of doing housework, women spent an average 2.6 hours; men – an average 2 hours. In a day, 48% of women and 20% of men did housework. Food preparation and clean-up is done by 65% of women and 39% of men.

Others are spending a couple of hours relaxing at a beach bar in Ibiza, or at the Cairns Lagoon in Australia

We spend an average of 2 hours at a beach bar. Cairns Esplanade in North Queensland, includes swimming in the Lagoon, and has beaches and theme parks.

YouTube said - find the weak spot and it falls apart with a tap from a sponge. Better fun than washing them all.

My seat

If we could hypnotise our spouse to do anything, we'd ...
1st choice: Get them to clean the house
2nd choice: Give us a massage

1 in 3 of us:
Claims a messy home is damaging our sex life
Thinks a clean house is one of our greatest pleasures
Wishes our partner wasn't so messy
Doesn't clean the bathroom in 6 months

Life is like a roll of toilet paper. The closer you get to the end, the faster it goes.

Women:
2.6 hours

She'd nearly mastered cleaning her son's bedroom.

4 out of 5 of us dread cleaning their rooms, when our children go off to college or university.

This mess is a place!

By the time you put away your duster, a man is only half way through polishing the radiator of a Rolls-Royce

It takes one man five hours to polish a Rolls-Royce radiator when making the car at its manufacturing plant in Goodwood, West Sussex, England.

Someone's on a New Orleans Paddle Wheeler Cruise, listening to jazz and enjoying a Creole dinner

A Paddle Wheeler Jazz Cruise is about 2.5 hours.

She'd spent all day on her 'Perfect Housewife' look. Pity about the cat asleep in the doorway.

It's about the same amount of time you'll share with your kids in the week, reading

Parents spend 2 hours 20 minutes a week reading to their children.

"Where's Hermione?" Harry asked Ron.

89

And soon you can choose – the housework or a quick pop over to Sydney, Australia for a bit of retail therapy (tough choice ...)

Virgin Galactic estimate their spaceplane could travel from London to Sydney in 2.5 hours, with looking down on Earth and zero-gravity fun.

If the shelves are dusty and the pots don't shine, it's because I've got better things to do with my time.

Men:
2.0 hours

"OK. OK. I'll make sure I replace the loo roll from now on!"

The top 3 bathroom woes:
3   leaving toothpaste drips in the sink
2   leaving up the loo seat
1   a clear winner ...

The Americans are doing 7,200,000 loads of laundry

Every second, 1,000 loads of laundry are started in America; an average of 350 loads a year per household.

50% of women are attracted to a guy who can do laundry.

"Santa, Dear, my crisp white apron is now pink. Did you wash it with your red suit again?!"

And North American guys are learning how to master that iron

In a survey, 7,878 American men and 800 Canadian men hurt themselves each year doing their ironing.

You could be spending half the time working out with the hoover

It's an average of an hour to vacuum the house.

Ironing wasn't her strong point either, but he seemed to love her anyway.

This house is protected by killer dust bunnies.

"Want a good workout, Darling?" she purred. Jim was about to find out how to use the hoover ...

"Well, at least we got him off the sofa."

While your pal is working out at the gym

Men spend 1.9 hours on sports, exercise or recreation a day.

13% of us exercise at home to watch what we want on TV.

And then you could lose maybe 200 calories on the bar billiard table – or cooking

A 68 kg/150 lb person loses 93 calories an hour - as a bartender, playing billiards or cooking.

91

And 2 out of 3 of you guys have already bartered yourselves a good deal for your time of being a 'new man' around the house

60% of women have to bribe their partners to do things round the house – with 'treats' like a night out with the guys, watching his favourite TV show, or a new gadget or tool.

"This programme contains strong scenes of a sexual nature throughout ... you'll be delighted to know."

WARNING

⊙ ⊙ ⊙ ⊙ ⊙ ⊙ ⊙

WHILE YOU'RE ... ANSWERING YOUR FOUR-YEAR-OLD'S QUESTIONS

12.5 : hours

A four-year-old child asks an average of 437 questions a day which, from 7.29 am (wake-up time) to 7.59 pm (bedtime) is a question every 2 minutes 36 seconds – about 23 questions an hour. Girls ask the most questions - about one every 2 minutes (1 minute 56 seconds).

And the 23 questions an hour is:
1 more than Prime Minister's Question Time (GB): 22
4 more than a Primary School Teacher: 19
5 more than doctors and nurses: 18

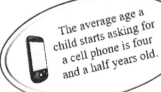

The average age a child starts asking for a cell phone is four and a half years old.

"Off to bed, Sweetie. Nighty-night."
"Why? Why is there a bed?
Why is it night? Why is it dark?
Why is there sky? Why me?"

92

A dragonfly, in the Cotswolds Water Park in England, is half way through its life

A dragonfly has a lifespan of 24 hours.

There's a *Dragonfly* Maze in Bourton-on-the-Water, the 'Little Venice' of the English Cotswolds; and there's a British Dragonfly Society.

In the Bay of Fundy, Canada, the water is now at the level of one of the highest tides in the world

The highest tides in the world are in the Bay of Fundy between Nova Scotia and New Brunswick on the east coast of Canada. The two daily high tides are 12 hours apart, when the water level rises to 14.5 to 16m/47 to 53 ft – about the height of a 5-storey house.

In Ontario, Canada, a Little Brown Bat has been having its daytime sleep in a tree

The bats can sleep 12 to 19 hours non-stop in the daytime.

You've a 1 in 20 trillion chance that you'll be hit by any of the 52,936.04 kg/52.1 tons of meteoroids bombarding Earth's atmosphere

Our atmosphere is showered every 24 hours by up to 101,605 kg/100 tons of meteoroids - fragments of dust and gravel and sometimes even big rocks (NASA Science News). The odds of being directly hit by a meteor are 1 in 20,000,000,000,000.

Meteoroids are 'meteors' when they enter Earth's atmosphere. If they don't burn up, they're called a 'meteorite'.

There are impact craters on Jupiter's moon, Callisto, and our own moon, as well as on Earth. The Vredefort crater in South Africa, 380 km/236.12 miles across, is 2,023 billion years old.

Meteorite fragments have been found in ancient Egyptian jewellery from 3,300 BC; one found in the Sahara is a new type of Mars rock.

If the '2011 AG5' body hits Earth in 2040, the odds of dying in that apocalypse are 1 in 12,500.

And over 300 million people looked for answers on 'cosmic' Wikipedia

There are 18 billion page views a month on Wiki, making 600 million a day, 25 million an hour and 312.5 million in the 12.5 hours. Wiki has over 5.1 billion users for over 58 million pages. The highest user is USA (25%), then Japan (5.97%), UK (5.38%) and Germany (5.13%). A main belt asteroid (274301) was officially renamed 'Wikipedia', by the Committee for Small Body Nomenclature, in January 2013, taking Wiki into the cosmos.

We've come from:
387 BC: Plato's 'Academy' school started in Athens - *to* …
2001: 15th January - Wikipedia launched on the World Wide Web. And then went from cyberspace into cosmic space in 2013.

WHILE YOU'RE … LOOKING FOR THINGS YOU'VE LOST

6.25 : days

We each spend over 150 hours (6.25 days) a year looking for things misplaced.

"Have a place for everything and keep the thing somewhere else – this is not a piece of advice, it is merely a custom."
Mark Twain

Americans bought 280 million Ritz Crackers, and ate

"No, Darling. I never give this number out. I only have this phone to call my cell phone so I can find it."

14,741,750 kg /833.75 g/32.5 million lbs of pickles - in the time you've been looking for your socks, wallet, slippers, purse, keys …

In the USA, they buy just under 45 million Ritz Crackers every day (281.25 million in 6.25 days) and eat 2,358,720 kg/5,200,000 lbs of pickles daily.

94

You could have had 150 phone sessions with American oracles to find your missing things

1 in 25 of the US population makes their living as a psychic.
Phone sessions average an hour, with 150 hours in 6.25 days.

"The best way to predict your future is to create it." *Abraham Lincoln*

Your stuff might have disappeared through a wormhole and zoomed 161.5 billion metres/100,500 million miles

Physicists believe wormholes – shortcuts through space and time - exist all around us but they're smaller than an atom. Some think they're related to the speed of light – 299,792,458 metres per second/186,000 miles a second - and there's 540,000 seconds in 6.25 days.

But you'll also spend the same amount of time in the year sorting out what-goes-with-what in clothes

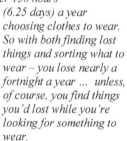

The average person spends just under 150 hours (6.25 days) a year choosing clothes to wear. So with both finding lost things and sorting what to wear – you lose nearly a fortnight a year ... unless, of course, you find things you'd lost while you're looking for something to wear.

"All you can hear is my voice. Now - where did you put the key to the Executive washroom?"

And you've had 437,500 thoughts go through your head

That's not 400,000-plus thoughts of 'where the ***** is it' or 'I can't have put weight on ... this dress/shirt must have shrunk'. The average person has 70,000 thoughts a day – about everything.*

WHILE YOU'RE ... WEARING OUT A PILLOW

1.5 : years

The typical lifespan of a pillow is 18 months.

The to's and 'fro's' (and '2's' and '4's) of Pillows
Women – like 4 pillows at home; and 1 in 2 takes their own pillow with them when they travel.
Men – prefer 2 pillows at home; and 1 in 4 of them takes their own pillow with them when they travel.

Snuggled against her pillow, Lucy liked to write love poems.

They're putting the last brush-stroke of paint onto the Eiffel Tower

"I love the way you hum
And I'd like to tickle your ..."
"Hmm ... what rhymes with 'hum'?"

With 7 million visitors a year, it's painted every 7 years by 25 painters, over 15 to 18 months, with 54,431.1 kg/60 tons of brown paint in three shades – the darkest being at the bottom.

The Tower was yellow in the 1890s. It was the world's tallest structure from 1889 until the New York Chrysler Building of 1930. It sways during a storm, and the iron expands in hot sun to make it 6"/2.54 cm bigger.

This is the longest painting job I've ever had!

All your usual elevators – at work, in the mall, and in apartment blocks – are each running 30,056 km/18,676.16 miles – the same as three quarters round the equator

Each year, an elevator runs a distance equivalent to half the circumference of the equator – half of 40,075.16 km/24,901.55 miles.

And you could be half way through a blue moon

A 'blue moon' is a full moon that happens twice in one month. Usually there's one full moon a month but, if there are more days in the calendar month than the moon's cycle of 29.5 days, the moon can rise at the beginning and end of a month. This can be every 33 months - about every 3 years. So you could say you're changing your pillow 'once in a blue moon'.

BLUE MOON

96

On average, we clean it out once every 2 years - though we clean the inside of the car twice a month.

We've orbited to our closest point to Mars, and could fly there in 8 months

Every two years, Mars and Earth are at their closest point ('opposition') – 55,000,000 km/35,000,000 miles apart. The time it takes for spacecraft to reach Mars at this time - in the range of 100 to 300 days depending on speed and alignment - is an average of 225 days – 8 months.

A man claiming to be a Martian lost his court case against Britain after a judge ruled that aliens have no rights. The man claimed government officials were plotting to kill him.

1 in 5 of us would try to befriend an alien from outer space if one came along.

In the Gulf of Corcovado, Chile, a baby Blue Whale has gone from 2,721.55 kg/3 tons to 71,654.1 kg/nearly 79 tons

In the first year of its life, the baby whale has over 227.31 litres/50 gallons of mother's milk a day and gains about 90.7 kg/200 lbs each day. It goes from 2,721.55 kg/6,000 lbs/3 tons at birth, adding 33,105.5 kg/73,000 lbs, to be 35,827.05 kg/79,000 lbs/39.5 tons in a year – 13.16 times its birth weight; and 71,654.1 kg/157,970.25 lbs/78.99 tons in two years.

Lee and Perrins Worcestershire Sauce is now ready to add to your Spaghetti Bolognaise

The ingredients in Lea and Perrins Worcestershire Sauce are stirred together and allowed to sit for two years before being bottled at the Midland Road factory in Worcester, England.

Culinary Success

Lea & Perrins' Sauce

97

On the African savannah, an elephant is finally giving birth

An elephant can be pregnant for 2 years.

That condom you've had stashed away is about to be chancy

The average shelf-life of a latex condom is two years.

A man's clocked up 888.36 km/552 miles driving around lost, refusing to ask for directions

Men clock up an average 444.18 km/276 miles a year aimlessly driving around lost rather than asking for directions; women drive around lost for 411.99 km/256 miles

After being lost on country roads for four hours with his map reading, she suddenly saw a road sign.

a year. A quarter of men wait over 30 minutes before asking directions; 12% refuse any help at all.

In an Indian mangrove forest, a Bengal Tiger cub has learnt to be independent

Tiger cubs will stay with their mothers in a family group for two years, until the cubs are able to survive on their own.

It could be an Olympic year

There are two sorts of Olympic Games – summer and winter – and they're each held every four years. From 1994, the IOC changed from having both in the same year to them alternating 2 yearly on even-numbered years, with the Summer Olympics in the leap year.

The library at Indiana University has sunk another 5 cm/2 inches

It sinks over 2.5 cm/1 inch every year because, on building it, the engineers didn't account for the weight of all the books that would be in it.

98

We could wrap the world in Velcro – four times
Every year, we make enough Velcro to stretch twice around the world.

You'll say goodbye to your old umbrella...
You'll use one for just over 2 years before it breaks.

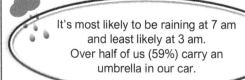

It's most likely to be raining at 7 am and least likely at 3 am. Over half of us (59%) carry an umbrella in our car.

"Rain ... Pish, Posh!" said Mary. "Umbrellas are far better used for flying."

... while there are 50,400 umbrellas travelling around lost on British transport
Approximately 25,200 umbrellas are lost each year on the British transport system. Or – to put it another way – think about the Centre Court at Wimbledon and imagine it with the retractable roof closed over it, like one huge umbrella. All the lost

umbrellas would be more than six and a half times deep all over it.

Whether the weather be fine,
Whether the weather be not,
Whether the weather be cold,
Whether the weather be hot,
We'll weather the weather,
Whatever the weather,
Whether we like it or not.

Spending Time
Money & Shopping

"We moved all the stuff that's bad for you to the top shelf."

Spending Time
Money & Shopping

When a customer gathers up his or her belongings, after completing shopping at a supermarket checkout, it takes an average 3.17 seconds.

Just two things will improve a woman's mood: 'I love you' and '50% discount'.

I will carry every grocery bag, or die trying, before making two trips.

The Sun is over 11.5 billion kg/12.6 million tons lighter when you head for the exit

The Sun loses 3.6 billion kg/4 million tons every second – losing over 11.5 billion kg/12.6 million tons in 3.17 seconds.

And 10,052 bananas are being nibbled

Worldwide, 100 billion are eaten in a year – 3,170.98 a second.

The 5 most consumed fruits worldwide are: tomatoes, bananas, watermelons, apples and grapefruit.

Going at 96.56 km/h/60 mph, a car's travelled over a length and a half of an Olympic swimming pool

A car moving at 96.56 km/h/60 mph covers 26.82 m/88 feet a second. So in 3.17 seconds, it's moved 85.02 m/278.96 feet. And an Olympic swimming pool is 49.99 m/164 feet long.

And the 75 metre freestyle gold goes to Mr Robinson in his sports coupé.

In a West Virginia garden, a Ruby-throated Hummingbird is flapping its wings 150 times

A Ruby-throated Hummingbird, hovering in open space, has a wing-beat rate of 50 to 52 times a second.

Hummingbirds are the only bird that can also fly backwards, but they can't walk. They consume half their weight in sugar each day.

Americans are buying 75 pieces of KFC chicken

25 pieces of KFC 'Original Recipe' are sold in the USA each second.

And nine Barbie dolls have been sold

Every second, three Barbie dolls are sold somewhere in the world, with 94 million sold each year – 40% of all doll sales.

"I heard you had a special offer on can openers ...."

☺ ☺ ☺ ☺ ☺ ☺ ☺ ☺

WHILE YOU'RE ... COMPLAINING ABOUT BAD SERVICE

8 : minutes

We spend eight minutes every day complaining about bad service (poll by Hilary Blinds).

Wednesday, 12 noon – is the best time to call customer service – when it's least busy.

A ray of sunlight has reached the Earth - for the 'light to dawn' on someone you're complaining to ...

It takes just over 8 minutes for light to get from the Sun to the Earth - at the speed of light.

COMPLAINT DEPARTMENT

TAKE A NUMBER

102

... and for them to 'see the light' of your complaint

My karma ran over your dogma.

It takes approximately 5, of the 8 minutes, for the eye to adapt from darkness to bright sunlight.

Someone's having a moan about the weather

A survey of 2,000 Brits found they complain about the weather 4 times a day for a total average of 8 mins 21 seconds. The 25 to 34 years old moaned the most; but a quarter of adults just got on with things despite the weather.

Into each life some rain must fall ... usually on weekends.

Woman: "Darling, I'll sit in the car till the rain stops while you set up the picnic."

And a woodpecker is also making its point - 9,600 times

Woodpeckers can peck 20 times a second and up to 12,000 times a day. Their brains are protected by shock-absorbing muscles – they can peck with a force of 1,200 g/2.65 lbs with each strike. That's like us striking our head against a wall at a speed of 25 km/h/16 mph each time (not recommended!).

☼ ☼ ☼ ☼ ☼ ☼ ☼ ☼

WHILE YOU'RE ... GROCERY SHOPPING

The Time Use Institute survey: we spend an average of 41 minutes per trip on grocery shopping.

41 : minutes

The least popular days for grocery shopping are Monday (women) and Thursday (men). *We ignore 99.3% of the items in a grocery store.*
2 out of 3 women use a well-worn and well-loved purse – never cleaning it.

"Well, you wanted to budget, so I bought all the 3 for 2 offers."

You could get your car tyres changed

It'll take you about 45 minutes to change tyres on a car, while others are battling the shopping cart with the wheel with a mind of its own.

While, in London, 62 parking tickets are being issued

There's 91 issued in an hour.

"I'm sorry about the parking, Officer. I washed my car this morning, and I can't do a thing with it."

"I regard golf as an expensive way of playing marbles." G K Chesterton

You've burnt off nearly 90 calories – which you could do, instead, hang gliding or playing golf

A 68 kg/150 lb person uses the same number of calories per hour golfing (using a golf cart), hang gliding, in child-care (bathing, feeding, etc) and food shopping with a cart – 130 calories an hour and 89 calories for 41 minutes.

You could be at a cocktail party, a retro rally or a friend's BBQ instead of deciding on what veg you need

We spend an average of 43.5 minutes over weekends and weekdays in socializing – visiting friends or attending or hosting social events.

Or – take a pneumatic drill through the centre of the Earth to a different continent

If you could drill a tunnel straight through the Earth, travelling through it - you'd reach the other side in 42 minutes 12 seconds.

Only one shopping day left till tomorrow.

WHILE YOU'RE ... OFFERING A MAN'S ADVICE ON YOUR LADY'S OUTFIT

1 : hour

A man will spend about an hour in total, each year, helping his wife or girlfriend to pick out an outfit.

What a Girl Needs

Spends £570/$737 a year on shoes

Owns 20 pairs but wears only 5 regularly

Has a pair she's never worn (86%)

"Give a girl the right shoes, and she can conquer the world."
Marilyn Monroe

"All I said was 'Do you really need *another* black coat'."

No woman ever said she didn't need to go shopping because she had enough clothes.

"Well?" she said to her husband. **"What do you think? Go on. Be honest."**

You've chosen way too wrong - if you've hit the shops on Christmas Eve

The busiest shopping hour for the Christmas holiday season is December 24 between 3 and 4 in the afternoon.

Christmas is a race to see which gives out first – your money or your feet.

Instead, you could be floating above the peaceful countryside in a hot air balloon

Flights can last about an hour; the whole experience of the occasion can take up to four hours.

105

You could shed some frustration on a nearby wall – and get slim

Banging you head against a wall uses 150 calories an hour – though not recommended!

Or polish your shoes with industrial quantities of elbow-grease

It takes 30 minutes a shoe to shine them military style.

Or do half your daily longbow practice

In England, by law - all men over the age of 14 must carry out two hours of longbow practice a day.

And then play safe by claiming you 'can't see the true beauty of her outfit because it's too dark'

It takes us 40 minutes to an hour to see in the dark.
When our eyes have adapted to it, they're 10,000 to a million times more sensitive than in daylight. People with blue eyes can see better in the dark, and those who are colour blind have excellent night vision.

Inside a woman's wardrobe, there's …

A dress a size too small as an incentive to lose weight *(80% of women)*
A little black dress that'll be there for 11 years *(80% of women)*
A handbag, accessory or outfit that her partner thinks is much cheaper than it really cost *(50% of women)*

WHILE YOU'RE ... STUCK IN QUEUES

2 : hours

A study of 2,000 Brits revealed that, in a week, they spend 17 minutes queueing for a toilet; 19 minutes for food and drinks on a night out; 29 minutes in line in the supermarket and 60 minutes in traffic – just over 2 hours a week (125 minutes) and up to 4.5 days a year just waiting.

Some days you're the pigeon, and some days you're the statue.

After weeks camping out for the Black Friday Sale at the clock store, nobody wanted to tell him it finished exactly 18 minutes ago.

Someone's ambled two thirds of the way round Stanley Park in Vancouver

A casual walk along Stanley Park Seawall in Vancouver, Canada (9.66 km/6 miles) takes about 3 hours.

A humanoid, on a planet in our Milky Way, could also be waiting in line for up to 486 hours

Astronomers think that 6% of all dwarf stars (the most common in the Universe) may host Earth-like planets. Some exoplanets are only 13 light-years away, and there's at least 17 billion Earth-sized exoplanets in the Milky Way. One of them (KOI-172.02) orbits a star similar to our Sun and could have alien life doing what we're doing right now. Here are the equivalent times humanoids could be waiting for two Earth hours on other planets, with the planet's equivalent to our daily 24 hours in brackets. On Mercury - 117.3 hours (1,408); Venus – 486 hours (5,832); Mars – 2.1 hours (25); Jupiter – 0.8 hours (10); Saturn – 0.9 hours (11); Uranus – 1.4 (17); and Neptune – 1.3 hours (16).

Mute swans have flown from Richmond, London to Oxford along the river Thames

They fly at 80.5- 88.5 km/h/50 -55 mph. The 160.9 km/ 100 mile route along the Thames would take 28 hours for us on foot.

107

WHILE YOU'RE ... DITCHING JUNK MAIL

3 : days

We spend the equivalent of three days a year in sorting and disposing of junk mail – 1.5 trees-worth per person of which 46% is never read.

"Just a few questions for Cooper's Direct Mail survey ... Did you come down here (a) to get away from junk mail, (b) it was the only place we wouldn't find you, or (c) both of the above?"

Nearly 400,000 people have been using the Brooklyn Bridge in New York City

Daily, 125,000 motor vehicles, 4,000 pedestrians and 2,600 cyclists (totalling 131,600 people – assuming one person for each car and bike) cross the Brooklyn Bridge..

The average clerk has produced 24 times the amount of junk mail – in waste paper

A clerk produces 2 kg/4.6 lb of waste paper a day. The 114.7 million American households receive 3,628,738,960 kg/4 million tons of junk mail a year – that's 31.75 kg/70 lbs and 0.09 kg/0.19 lb a day per household. So a clerk produces 24.2 times more waste paper a day than an average American household receives in junk mail.

His Majesty
The Palace

And His Majesty the King has received 750 more letters from his public

The King receives 200 to 300 letters from the public every day – an average of 250 letters a day.

> **"We already have everything we need."**
> *Pema Chödrön*

WHILE YOU'RE ... PAYING FOR WHAT YOU BOUGHT ON EBAY

1 : week

The normal time for paying for purchases on eBay is 7 days.

Shopping Data

1 in 4 of us is most influenced in what we buy by word of mouth.

'Old age' is when we stop shopping – according to a survey of 'seniors'.

38 million of us have been on the toilet while we've been

It was the moment that Bob realised he'd picked the wrong hat size on eBay.

Buy your new bedroom suite from us, and we will stand behind it for six months.

About half of America has lived off plastic

In the US, almost 45% of people don't use cash in a week.

American Money

Every person in the US has an average of two credit cards; and 97% of American paper money contains traces of cocaine.

A dollar can be made into small change in 293 ways.

725.2 square kilometres/280 square miles of land around the world has been changed into desert

Worldwide, 103.6 square kilometres/40 square miles of land is changed, each day, into a desert of sand.

For Sale - Pole suitable for Pole Leaning (like Pole Dancing but less energetic).

"I spy with my little eye something beginning with 'S'"

109

A house fly is half-way through its life
A house fly lives for 14 days. Flies cruise at 8 km/h/5 mph.

A new-born kitten will have its first dream
Kittens begin dreaming at just over one week old.

And in the Himalayas, a bamboo has grown 6.3 metres/21 feet
Bamboo can grow at least 0.9 m/3 ft in a 24 hour period.

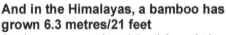

Always borrow from a pessimist – he doesn't expect to be paid back.

"Honey, I've got the stuff from eBay, so I can unblock the toilet now."

Someone bought the surprise package on eBay.

"Imperfection is beauty, madness is genius and it's better to be absolutely ridiculous than absolutely boring." *Marilyn Monroe*

Time Off
Indoor Leisure

"I'm going to set this lot up – will contain scenes that some may find upsetting and strong language throughout."

111

Time Off
Indoor Leisure

WHILE YOU'RE ... PLAYING A GAME OF BACKGAMMON

20 : minutes

The board game Backgammon lasts for approximately 20 minutes.

A Mako Shark has swum 32.2 km/20 miles

A Mako Shark can swim at a top speed of 96.56 km/h/60 mph when looking for food – which is 32.2 km/20 miles in 20 minutes.

You could be watching an episode of 'Friends'

Shows average 20 to 23 minutes – the commercials make them into 30 minute programmes. Of the 236 episodes, the pilot was on 22nd September 1994; the final programme was on 6th May 2004.

Mike hoped Jane wouldn't realise that he was making up the rules of Strip Backgammon as he went along.

A man is cleaning up the kitchen after serving a snack and a drink

Men spend just over 20 minutes a day on food and drink preparations and cleaning up in the kitchen.

"My goodness! That was some oven cleaner, Ernest!"

A fully-loaded super tanker has been in stop mode the whole time

Travelling at a normal speed of 12 to 16 knots, it takes about 20 minutes for it to stop. They gather huge momentum when sailing, so most turn off their engines 25 km/15.5 miles before they dock.

112

WHILE YOU'RE ...
WATCHING THE NEWS
ROUND-UP ON TV

A TV News show usually lasts 30 minutes.

It's the same amount of time you spent as the first speck of life, to be a part of the cosmos unfolding before you on the TV ...

Every human being spent 30 minutes as a single cell.

... while a new galaxy is being 'born' 28,000 lifetimes away, to exist millions of years from now

Two galaxies – VV340 North and VV340 South, known together as Arp 302 - are colliding 450 million light years from Earth in the constellation of Bootes. In millions of years, they will merge and form a new galaxy. Due to the way the two galaxies are aligned, they're known as 'The Cosmic Exclamation Mark'. It would take 4,473 years to travel a light year in the Helios Probes at 241,401.6 km/h/150,000 mph, and 2,012,850 years to travel to Arp 302, or 1,057,953,960,000 minutes to watch the birth of that galaxy – 35,265,132,000 times longer than when you began life and 28,755 lifetimes of 70 years.

"We are all in the gutter, but some of us are looking at the stars." *Oscar Wilde*

113

Women – take up to 20 minutes to choose dessert (7 out of 10)
Men – choose twice as fast as women from a menu

"Waiter, there's a fly in the butter!" "Yes Sir, it's a butterfly!"

With a magnum of wine, they toasted the cook, the waiters, the delivery man who brought the food – twice, the vegetable grewer – I mean – grower, the orchyestra, the par cark attendleby, and the candidoodly thingy stuck in the tiddle of the mable.

 Food Figures

70% of us order the same thing when we're at our favourite restaurant.
43% of single women go on a date to get a free meal.
175 calories – we eat less if a restaurant has soft music and low lights.

Firemen are on standby in Chicago, Auckland, Manchester, Cape Town and Lyon ...

... and most cities and towns around the world, having a 24 hour fire service. So you're covered for your one hour meal.

In Chicago, it's illegal to eat in a place if it's on fire.

With his third unsuccessful batch of moonshine whiskey exploding in flames, if ever Geoff needed a drink, it was now.

You're over 100 calories in hand - if you had an hour's sex before you got to the restaurant

Estimates are that a 58.97 kg/130 lb woman burns 70-120 calories an hour during sex; and a 77.11 kg/170 lb man burns 77 to 155 calories. In one survey, sex was most popular before a big meal.

"Wow!" she said. "What an evening! Sex - and spare calories for dessert!"

Roses are red, violets are blue,
Vodka costs less than dinner for two.

Practise safe eating –
always use condiments.

Your favourite soap opera characters have totalled up 6 lies

In an hour of a soap opera, there are 6.2 lies. J R Ewing, 'Dallas': "'Never tell the truth when a good lie'll do!" The 'Who Done It?" episode of Dallas, on November 21, 1980, watched by over 350 million worldwide, revealed who shot J R. The shooter? Kristin Shepard (Mary Crosby), J R's sister-in-law.

And two lots of tourists have been gazing at London's cityscape

The London Eye completes one rotation in 30 minutes, travelling at 26 cm/10.2 inches a second or 0.9 km/h/0.6 mph – twice the speed of a tortoise. The wheel and capsules weigh as much as 1,272 London black cabs (2,100,000 kg/2,100 tonnes). It's as tall as 64 British red phone boxes piled up (135m/147.64 yards). With good visibility you can see 40 km/25 miles to Windsor Castle; and it can carry 800 passengers for each trip (the same number as 11 red London busses).

WHILE YOU'RE ... HAVING A PIANO LESSON

1 : hour

For an adult, a lesson is an hour.

Ommmm

In Canada, Japan, and other countries, dogs are enjoying an hour of music at their own yoga class

Owners attend an hour's 'Doga' classes – a yoga class for dogs – in USA, England, Hong Kong, Japan and Canada.

"Hmm, I don't know," she said. "Can we try it in the upstairs front bedroom, again?"

In Britain, you've an 80% chance that the piano you're using is out of tune

1,800,000 of the 2,250,000 pianos in Britain are out of tune at any given moment.

And you could play 'Flight of the Bumblebee' 30 times

Composed in 1899 by Rimsky-Korsakov, the short version takes about two minutes; the opera version – three minutes, 55 seconds.

🕐 🕐 🕐 🕐 🕐 🕐 🕐

WHILE YOU'RE ... WATCHING A BALL GAME

1-3 : hours

"It is not the critic who counts; not the man who points out how the strong man stumbles, or where the doer of deeds could have done them better. The credit belongs to the man who is actually in the arena, whose face is marred by dust and sweat and blood."

Theodore Roosevelt

American Football Game/ Hockey Match: 1 hour

Professional and college American Football games last 60 minutes- not counting breaks, although research shows that a typical NFL game is 5.9% of actual playing time. A field hockey match lasts 60 minutes, as does an ice hockey match (both excluding breaks).

The ref was either brave or bonkers to try out a red card on 'The Crusher'.

The sports mistress *really* wanted to win this match: *"Whack 'em on the bum, Girls! Go for their shins! Debag 'em! Trip 'em up!"*

For 1 in 9 guys – it's an extra hour too much for their relationship

1 in 9 men are dumped by a woman because of how much sport they watch.

And for 1 in 4 married men, the hour could mean sleeping on the sofa or alone

With 23% of married women, their number one complaint is their partner pays more attention to sports than to them.

Husband for sale. Remote included.

"The wife's at her mother's. Said 'you can have your Big Match' and off she went." "So back to yours for kick-off, then?"

It's time for your 4 chicken wings

1.4 billion chicken wings are eaten on Super Bowl Sunday. The USA population, over 5 years old and who might eat the chicken wings, is 305.9 million. With dividing the 1.4 billion chicken wings by the 305.9 million Americans, each American eats 4.6 chicken wings watching the Super Bowl.

"What fun!" laughed Karen. "Let's see what I can hit if I throw it over arm next time?"

To Check the Score
1 in 5 men sneak away from a date
1 in 8 sneaks out of a wedding

By half-time, someone's finished their game at the local bowling alley

It's about 15 minutes for one bowler to bowl one game; two bowlers – 30 minutes, with an average number of strikes.

By half-time, a giraffe in Kenya, has finished its daily sleep

Giraffes sleep for five minutes at a time, and an average of 30 minutes a day.

And, by the final whistle, nearly 7,000 people have bought an Apple iPad

Apple sold 61 million iPads in 2022 – averaging 6,963.5 in an hour.

Rugby Match: 1 hour 20 minutes

A rugby match, without breaks, should take 80 minutes in total.

A great birthday present?
4 out of 5 men would choose tickets to see their favourite sport team.

Eh! What's going on?!

You never give up the ball, so we brought our own.

It's the same amount of time that you'll be targeted by commercials today

You'll spend 81 minutes a day watching or listening to ads.

By half time, a patient has had their tonsils removed in hospitals around the world – Florence, Perth, Islamabad, Frankfurt …

A tonsillectomy operation takes 30 to 60 minutes - an average of 45 minutes, not including healing time.

"I've checked, Sir, and no! Now you're fully recovered, your health insurance will not pay for my nurses to visit you daily to give you bed baths till your shower's fixed."

> The two hardest things to handle in life are failure and success.

Football (Soccer) Match: 1.5 hours
A football match, without breaks, is 45 minutes each way.

A person who aims at nothing is sure to hit it.

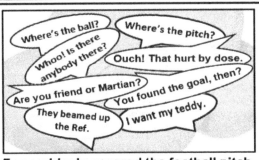

Where's the ball?

Where's the pitch?

Whoo! Is there anybody there?

Ouch! That hurt by dose.

Are you friend or Martian?

You found the goal, then?

They beamed up the Ref.

I want my teddy.

Fog suddenly covered the football pitch.

Your female partner is enjoying her own fitness and friendships

In a day, women spend 1.4 hours on sports, exercise or recreation.

Coffee-bar gossip

90% of men are attracted to a woman when she's sweaty.

At a swimming pool in Tubingen, Germany, they removed the mirrors from the changing rooms. Women got dressed three times faster.

Someone on the high-speed Taiwan train has covered the whole length of the country – 297.7 km/185 miles between Taipei and Kaohsiung

Taiwan High Speed Rail runs 345 km/ 214 miles along the west coast of the country, carrying 129,000 passengers

Very funny!

ONE WAY → ONE WAY ←

Who did that!

a day at a top speed of 300 km/h/186 mph (4.99 km/min/3.1 miles/min). It can cover the length of the country in 96 minutes.

And, if you fell asleep at kick-off, you'll be dreaming at the end of the game

The REM dream stage of sleeping starts about 90 minutes after falling asleep, recurring at 90 minute intervals. It's about 25% of sleeping time - and your brain is very active in REM sleep.

It is wise to keep in mind that no success or failure is necessarily final.

Baseball Game: 3 hours

The average length of a baseball game is 3 hours – with various reported time lengths of 2 to 4 hours.

30,000 people have passed through the doors of Harrods

Harrods is open most days for 10 hours. About 10,000 people an hour pass through Harrods' doors. On a busy day, over 100,000 can file through the store – the same as double the New York City stadium crowd of 50,000 and about the same as the 90,000-plus in the Los Angeles Memorial Coliseum.

You've probably sent one of the world's 62,499,960 tweets
5,787 tweets a second are sent, and 20,833,320 an hour worldwide.

Twittering Tweets
Users in millions: US 73, Japan 55.55, India 22.1, UK 17.55
Daily active users: 237.8 million worldwide, 80% on a mobile
Users: 43.6% female, 56.4% male, 25 to 34 years (38.5%)
Most used emoji: Laughing face with tears of joy – 75 countries

And a dolphin is peacefully half way through its daily sleep, in a lagoon in Hawaii
A dolphin sleeps an average 7 hours a day.

We shared a common ancestor (the Mesonycid) with dolphins 60 to 65 million years ago. And dolphins have names for each other that they respond to, like we do.

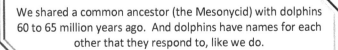

"Time you enjoy wasting is not wasted time." *Marthe Troly-Curtin*

WHILE YOU'RE ... PLAYING COMPUTER GAMES

4 : hours

The average gamer spends up to four hours a session playing video games. 45% of gamers are women. A third of the world's population are active gamers – the most in China and USA.

Meddle not in the affairs of Dragons, for you are crunchy and go good with ketchup.

If I've learned anything from video games it's that, when you meet enemies, it means you're going in the right direction.

It's the same amount of time that: an elephant in the grassland of Ghana, and a sheep in the South Island of New Zealand, and a cow in the fields of Ireland spend a day sleeping
They all sleep for four hours a day.

You could be giving your fondest rendition of 'Do-Re-Mi' in the 'Sound of Music' coach in Salzburg
The 'Sound of Music' tour lasts four hours.

Or you could tour the Opera House and take in the panorama of Sydney by sea plane
A four hour tour.

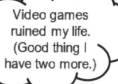

Video games ruined my life. (Good thing I have two more.)

122

WHILE YOU'RE ... CONSIDERING YOUR NEXT CHESS MOVE

3 : days

The time limit to make a move, following your opponent's, for an on-line chess game is 3 days or you forfeit the game.

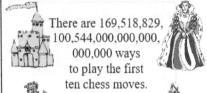

There are 169,518,829, 100,544,000,000,000, 000,000 ways to play the first ten chess moves.

Do you really *need* to breathe while I'm thinking?

Take measured risks: if you win, you will be happy; if you lose, you will be wise.

Someone's hiked through the magnificent wooded hills and coves of the Queen Charlotte Track in New Zealand

It takes 3 to 5 days to hike the 71 km/44 mile trail.

A walrus in the Bering Strait, and a rat in Naples, have swum non-stop during your time of deliberation

Walruses can swim for more than 3 days without stopping to sleep. They can sleep up to 19 hours at a time but, unlike most animals, they don't need to sleep every day. Some species of rats can tread water for 3 days. They can also swim 1.6 km/1 mile and jump 3 feet in the air.

North American elevators have moved 975 million people, and escalators - 735 million people

Each day, elevators move 325 million passengers, and escalators – 245 million passengers - of the 529 million people of North America. Elevators are 20 times safer than escalators, and safer than cars.

123

A gastrotrich, on the seashore of Karachi, Pakistan, has lived its life

A microscopic animal ('hairy back'), it's found in fresh water and marine environments. It has a 3 to 21 day lifespan.

And the Europa moon has orbited Jupiter

Europa is large, dense and icy and the smoothest object in our Solar System. It's smaller than the Earth's moon – 3,138 km/1,949.86 miles in diameter - and takes 3.55 Earth days to orbit Jupiter. There are 67 moons around Jupiter.

Gilbert Bohuslav, a chess and computer expert in Houston, Texas, taught his computer to play a good game of chess with him. Inspired by his success at this, and being a fan of Westerns, he then tried to teach his computer to write a Western story. Having fed into it the most-used words in Western movies, this was the result: "Tex Doe, the Marshall of Harry City, rode into town. He sat hungrily in the saddle, ready for trouble. He knew that his sexy enemy, Alphonse the Kid, was in town. The Kid was in love with Texas Horse Marion. Suddenly the Kid came out of the upended Nugget Saloon. "Draw, Tex," he yelled madly. Tex reached for his girl, but before he could get it out of his car, the Kid fired, hitting Tex in the elephant and the tundra. As Tex fell, he pulled out his own chess board and shot the Kid 35 times in the King. The Kid dropped in a pool of whisky. "Aha," Tex said. "I hated to do it but he was on the wrong side of the Queen." Gilbert settled for chess instead.

☉ ☉ ☉ ☉ ☉ ☉ ☉

WHILE YOU'RE ... WAITING FOR THE NEXT CGI ANIMATION

1 : year

It takes 4 to 6 months to have the storyboards and scripts ready for a CGI film, and 6 to 8 months to make it – averaging a year.

... and while they waited for frog's spell to work, bunny told them all a joke ...

I say, I say, I say ... What's a twain? It's what a wabbit wides on the wailway.

There were 10 billion Spam messages that never reached you

A year's worth of Spam, blocked by one Anti-Spam company, is 10 billion unwanted emails – almost 27.5 million a day and 318 each second.

In the Florida Everglades, an alligator has built up a nice appetite
Alligators can go without food for up to a year.

You've taken 15 trips to the Post Office
An adult goes to the Post Office an average of 15 times a year.

A young Formosan wrote 700 letters to his girlfriend. She is to marry the postman. *(Stoke Evening Sentinel, UK)*

In New York and Paris, lightning hit the Empire State Building and the Eiffel Tower about 25 times
Because lightning seeks out the highest object, the Empire State Building and the Eiffel Tower get struck by lightning 20 to 30 times a year. But each time lightning strikes some ozone gas is produced, so it's strengthening the ozone layer in our atmosphere.

A grey whale has swum over 16,093 km/10,000 miles - from Mexico to the Arctic seas
The grey whale has the longest annual migration of any mammal – 16,093 to 19,312 km/10,000 to 12,000 miles, between winter calving lagoons in the warm Mexican waters, along the Pacific coast, and to its summer feeding grounds of the cold Arctic sea.

In Hawaii, over 17 non-indigenous insects have made it their home

There is an average of 17.5 non-native insects entering Hawaii each year.

And it's 10 cm/4 inches closer to saying 'Aloha' to Japan
The oceanic plate under the Hawaiian chain is moving about 10 cm/4 inches a year to the North West – towards Japan.

125

Lego turned out over 300 million toy tyres

Lego makes 318 million of them each year - 870,000 every day – at its factory in Denmark.

We've generated up to 50 million tonnes/55 million tons of e-waste

In 2022, worldwide, we bought 386 million PCs, desktops and laptops, 163.2 million tablets, 202 million TVs, and 1.5 billion smartphones. Discarding the old electrical units, we create up to 50 millions of tonnes of waste every year. There's a huge criminal industry retrieving our bank passwords, credit card numbers, addresses and personal details from the e-waste, and selling the information - or 'demanding money with menaces' from people who owned the information. You have a 200 to 1 chance of having your identity stolen.

Almost the same number of babies were born in India as there are people in Australia

India has the highest number of births annually – 23 million (2022) - about 1 in 5 of all births worldwide. Australia's population (2022) was 26.1 million.

In the tropical rain forest of Mount Wai'ale'ale, on the island of Kauai, Hawaii, they only had five days without rain

Rainfall on Mount Wai'ale'ale can be up to 1,270 cm/500 inches a year – that's 12.7 m or 41.67 feet/13.89 yards of the wet stuff.

"I think they forecast a heavy downpour after this shower."

Americans consumed: 715 million

slices of pie, 40,914,827 litres/9 million gallons of Slurpees, 10 billion doughnuts, 3 billion pizzas – and each: 190 pieces of gum, 113.7 litres/25 gallons of milk, 54.4 kg/120 lb of potatoes and 9 kg/20 lb of apples.

They also bought 10 bottles of wine per household – but, as men bought 15 bottles a year - where did the other 5 bottles go?!

And they spent over $40 billion/£23.8 billion on their pets

It includes $3 billion/£1,787,310,000 on cat and dog food for the 100 million dogs and cats in the USA.

Part of the Family
2% of pets have their own Facebook page
2 out of 3 dogs have a sweater, winter coat or raincoat
54% of dogs have a gift more valuable than a partner's was
2 out of 3 letters and cards are from the pet and its owner

Did You Know?
The level of a cat's purring can help it heal itself. Cats (domestic and wild cats - cheetahs, pumas, ocelots etc) have 'therapeutic' frequencies of purring. These are best at 25 and 50 Hz and second best at 100 and 200 Hz, promoting bone strength by 30% and speeding up the healing of fractures.

The French ate more snails and cheese than any other country; the Turkish people drank most tea

The French eat 36,287,390 kg/40,000 tons of snails a year – averaging 500 snails per French citizen. And they eat 24.4 kg/53.8 lbs/3.8 stone of cheese per person per year – nearly double that of the Americans who average 13.6 kg/29.98 lbs/2.14 stone each. The biggest tea drinking nations, with the percentage of the population are: Turkey (90%), Ireland (69%) and Britain (59%). Tea is the second most widely consumed drink globally; water is the first.

And the Swiss got heavily into chocolate – 11.9 kg/26.24 lbs/1.8 stone each person

Second are the Irish at 9.9 kg/21.8 lbs each – and more than the Americans, Swedes, Danes, French and Italians; and third is the UK – 9.5 kg/20.9 lb per person which, with a regular chocolate bar being 40 to 45 g/1.4 to 1.6 oz, works out at 210 to 238 bars each in a year. USA Today reported that Americans collectively eat 45.4 kg/100 lbs – or 1,031.8 to 1,135 bars - of chocolate a second.

Time Out
Outdoor Leisure

"OK, so tomorrow it's mountain-biking, rock-climbing, swimming ... "

Time Out
Outdoor Leisure

WHILE YOU'RE ... WALKING THROUGH CENTRAL PARK

1 : hour

From north to south (the longest route), it's 60 minutes, and 4 minutes to drive it.

In the Arctic, a polar bear has walked nearly 1.5 km/1 mile more than you, on an

ice flow
It's 4.02 km/2.5 miles from north to south in Central Park. A polar bear walks at an average speed of 5.5 km/h/3.4 mph so, if walking continuously, has covered about 5.5 km/3.4 miles on the Arctic ice while you were in central New York.

Across the States, 250 acres of land is being used for urban development
In the USA, about 6,000 acres of open space is lost to urban development daily – 250 acres an hour/4 acres a minute.

SIT!

If you take your dog, you'll burn off 250 calories
You burn 252 calories an hour, walking with your dog.

And someone, somewhere, is getting a tattoo instead
A small simple quarter-size tattoo could take an hour.

| Tattoos done while you wait | 129

"Are you sure this time ...?"

WHILE YOU'RE ... CLIMBING MOUNT SNOWDON

It's 6 hours to walk up and down Mount Snowdon in Wales, UK.

The best view comes after the hardest climb.

It could be chill time

In an average day, a man spends 6 hours on leisure activities, including watching TV, exercising and socialising – and that could include drinking an average of three and a half litres/six pints on a Friday or Saturday night.

"Darling, if it helps us to reach the next ledge then, yes – you did turn the iron off at home."

The average hangover lasts 9 hours 45 minutes. 2 out of 3 men have had beer for breakfast.

A man from Kent, England, who'd given up the booze to lose some of his 88.9 kg/14 stone, won a 5-day break to a German Beer fest.

A Mayfly is living its whole lifetime in the Glacier National Park, Montana

The Mayfly lives only six hours, but its eggs take three years to hatch.

It's the equivalent of four months on the planet 55 Cancri E

It's thought that one year on the alien planet of 55 Cancri E lasts 18 hours of Earth's time. It's a super-hot extrasolar planet and one of five exoplanets orbiting a bright star named 55 Cancri in a solar system lying in the constellation of Cancer (The Crab). It's 41 light years from Earth. A third of the planet has pure diamonds.

130

A chimp, in a tree by the river Zaire in Tanzania, is spending the whole time foraging for food

Chimpanzees look for food six to eight hours a day.

Go out on a limb – the fruits out there.

A massage therapist is treating six clients

A relaxation massage last 50 to 60 minutes.

And 9.000 Americans are getting a passport

25 Americans get a passport in one minute (US Department of State) and 1,500 in an hour.

WHILE YOU'RE ... WATCHING A ONE-DAY INTERNATIONAL CRICKET MATCH

8 : hours

Normally one day, this may run over 8 hours and into a second day, if rain delays play. A Twenty20 match is usually 3 to 4 hours. Test cricket – 4 or 5 days.

In the Dominican Republic, someone who was married at the start of the match, is divorcing by close

of play
You can file for divorce

in a day there.

"Well, folks, it's now three hours since anyone hit the ball. Anyone want to try? Please. Umpire? Tea lady? You there – in the white hat with a picnic? Want to give it a go? I'll give you what cash I got. I'm dying of boredom here ... "

Your eye muscles will move 86,400 times

They move 3 times in a second. If the same muscular movement was applied to the legs, you'd be walking 69.2 km/43 miles in the 8 hours.

131

You could be on a tour of the Giza pyramids, Egyptian Museum and the Sphinx
Tours are usually 8 hours.

The sexual urge of the camel
Is greater than anyone thinks.
After several months on the desert,
It attempted a rape on the Sphinx.
Now, the intimate parts of that Lady
Are sunk 'neath the sands of the Nile.
Hence the hump on the back of the camel
And the Sphinx's inscrutable smile.
(Artillery Camp, Cairo, 1940)

In India, 14 million people are going to the movies, and the same number is travelling on the railways

14 million Indians go to the movies daily (about 1% of the 1.4 billion population) and pay the equivalent of an average Indian's day's wages (US $1-3/£0.50 to £1.50) to see one of the 800-plus films made each year by Bollywood (more than twice the number of US made feature films). And daily, 14 million people travel on the Indian Railways – over 6 million on the Mumbai Suburban section.

"This is your conductor speaking. Don't anyone sneeze on this bridge!"

And:

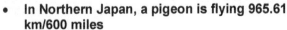
- **In Northern Japan, a pigeon is flying 965.61 km/600 miles**

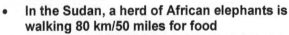
- **In the Sudan, a herd of African elephants is walking 80 km/50 miles for food**

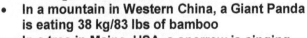
- **In a mountain in Western China, a Giant Panda is eating 38 kg/83 lbs of bamboo**

- **In a tree in Maine, USA, a sparrow is singing 2,000 times**

Pigeons can fly 965.61 km/600 miles a day over 12 hours, using the sun as a compass and the Earth's magnetic fields when the sun's obscured. In one race of this length from Japan, a pigeon got lost and ended up 8,046.7 km/5,000 miles away in Vancouver Island, Canada. Elephants normally walk a few miles a day, but can travel 80km/50 miles when food is scarce. An adult elephant in the wild can eat about 100 to 200 kg/220 to 440 lb of food and drink about 225 litres/49.49 gallons of water a day - sometimes continuously at 4 to 8 litres/7 to 14 pints a trunk-full. Giant Pandas can eat 38 kg/83 lbs of bamboo a day. A song sparrow in Maine sings more than 2,000 times a day.

WHILE YOU'RE ... SWIMMING THE ENGLISH CHANNEL

Tackling the 33.8 km/21 mile "Everest of open-water swimming" – just 10 % of those attempting it complete the crossing. The finishing times include the fastest swim at just over 7 hours and the slowest at nearly 27 hours – averaging 17 hours.

Being awake that long, you'll feel like you've had a shot of vodka

If you stay awake for 17 to 19 hours, you suffer a decrease in physical performance equivalent to a blood alcohol level of 0.05%. That's

like having one standard drink eg a 340 g/12 oz bottle of beer, a 142 g/5 oz glass of wine, or 42.5 g/1.5 oz

"Ooo! With all that muscle you'll easily cross the Channel," said Felicity. "An outboard motor might help," John muttered.

of 80 proof liquor, like vodka, tequila or rum – alone or in a mixed drink. 16% to 60% of road accidents involve this effect of sleep deprivation. Alcohol limits apply to operating some boats and jet-skis in GB, Australia and America. So don't offer to drive the boat back when you've finished your Channel swim ... as if you had the energy anyway!

Don't wait for your ship to come in – swim out to it.

You've swum 0.6 mm/0.024 ins more than you would have yesterday

The English Channel grows 300 mm/0.98 ft wider each year – 0.82 mm/0.032 ins a day and 0.58 mm/0.0019 ft/0.02 ins in 17 hours.

He who burns his bridges had better be a damn good swimmer.

Owl Monkeys in palm trees in Brazil have been asleep the whole time

They're the longest sleeping of the primates –17 hours a day.

But your cat will remember how long you've been out – if it can stay awake or it's not watching television

Tests conducted by the University of Michigan concluded that a cat's memory can last as long as 16 hours – more than that of monkeys and orang-utans. But cats also sleep for an average of 15 hours a day and are inclined to watch TV – more than dogs.

Feline Facts
A cat lives, on average, for 15 years.
It's in deep sleep for 15% of its life and light sleep for 50%. So a 15 year old cat has spent about 10 years of its life asleep. It spends 30% of its time self-grooming, leaving about 5% of its time for everything else, including eating.
40% of cats are ambidextrous; 60% - right or left 'pawed'.
Data's cat, Spot, in Star Trek 'The Next Generation' was played by six different cats.

And thou shalt have dominion over all the beasts – except, of course, the cats.

All the time you've been in the water – that's the time difference between Hong Kong and Alaska

Hong Kong is always 17 hours ahead of Alaska.

And 'the Scooter' triangle has completed a circuit around Neptune, while you've been swimming part of the Earth's Atlantic Ocean

When Voyager 2 visited Neptune, it filmed a small, irregular white triangle - 'the Scooter' - that zips around Neptune's surface every sixteen hours.

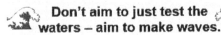
Don't aim to just test the waters – aim to make waves.

WHILE YOU'RE ... HIKING ROUND THE GRAND CANYON

It takes 4 to 6 days to hike the 70.81 km/44 miles round the Grand Canyon, Arizona – averaging 5 days.

May your trails be crooked, winding, lonesome, dangerous, leading to the most amazing view.
May your mountains rise into and above the clouds.

Your blood has circulated to every inch of your body 5,000 times

The heart circulates your blood around your body about 1,000 times each day.

Inside a nearby termite mound, the queen can produce 125,000 eggs

A termite queen can produce 20,000 to 30,000 eggs in a day – averaging 25,000 (1,041.67 an hour, 17.36 a minute). She can live for 45 years.

While a queen bee in an English woodland can lay 7,500 eggs

She can lay 800 to 1,500 eggs a day.

6 couples are getting married via the internet

Using Skype, a couple may marry by proxy, each in different places, via the internet – but only in Mexico, Paraguay and, in the USA - California, Colorado, Texas, Alabama and Montana. Through one US company there are 400 to 500 marriages a year; and averaging 450, that's 6 marriages in 5 days.

"Darling, my mother's here to celebrate our happy day!"

"And my ex-girlfriend's here to wish us luck."

135

And polar Eskimos on the Greenland ice are walking

over a ravine longer than the Grand Canyon and a mile below them

This canyon, revealed by a NASA mission, is 750 km/460 miles long and 800 m/2,600 feet/0.5 miles deep in places – like parts of the Grand Canyon. It's thought that water flowed in the Greenland canyon from the interior to the coast, and that it's older than the 4 million-year old ice sheet covering it. The Greenland Ice Sheet covers about 80% of Greenland and is the second largest ice body in the world, after the Antarctic Ice Sheet.

"Why do they call it Shady Holl ... Aahhh!"

"Do not go where the path may lead, go instead where there is no path and leave a trail."
Ralph Waldo Emerson

WHILE YOU'RE ... AT GLASTONBURY

5 : days

The Glastonbury Festival is 5 days in June, in Somerset, England.

Life is biodegradable art.

YOU ROCK

In nearby fields, cows are 'chatting' for longer than you – and with a Somerset drawl

Cows sleep for 4 hours a night and moo both night and day. So, unless you have 4, or less, hours' sleep, cows can be verbal over a longer period during the 5 days than you can. Cows can have regional accents. Farmers in Glastonbury consider their cows moo with a Somerset accent. Birds also have chirping accents distinctive to parts of the country.

The two suns of Kepler-16b have completed an eighth of their orbit, 105 million km/65 million miles away

The two suns of Kepler-16b, an extrasolar planet, have a 41 day orbit. The planet revolves around the two suns and is the most 'Tatooine-like' in our galaxy. Tatooine is the name of the home planet of Luke Skywalker and was created by George Lucas for the 'Star Wars' saga. The planet was a fictional harsh desert world orbiting two suns. Tatooine first featured in the 1977 film 'Star Wars' and visions of the binary sunset are an iconic image of the film series.

> **"If a man does not keep pace with his companions, perhaps it is because he hears a different drummer. Let him step to the music which he hears, however measured or far away."** *Henry David Thoreau*

The people of Iceland have drunk more Coca-Cola than you – 1.88 litres/3.3 pints each

Iceland consumes more Coca-Cola per capita than any other nation – averaging 136 litres/30 gallons/240 pints each a year, and 0.38 litres/0.66 pints a day each person..

500 million photos have been uploaded on Instagram

Nearly 100 million photos and videos are uploaded daily on Instagram.

> **"And those who were seen dancing were thought to be insane by those who could not hear the music."** *Friedrich Nietzsche*

It takes 4 days to ascend Everest from Base Camp and 2 days to return to Base Camp – excluding time spent at the top of the mountain.

About 3,000 people have reached the top of the 8,849.9 metre/29,035 foot/5.49 miles peak. Those who've been on the mountain have left over 90,718.5 kg/100 tons of trash.

With meeting the Abominable Snowman, Steve was about to set the fastest record for skiing down Everest backwards.

It's odds of 1 in 10 that you'll be alive at the end of the very chilling 6 days of your life

Breathe in. Breathe out. Breathe in. Breathe out. Forget this and attaining any goal will be the least of your problems.

You have a 1 in 10 chance of making the climb; there are 120 corpses on the mountain and 265 have died trying.

A blue whale in the warm Indian Ocean has eaten 32,658.66 kg/ 36 tons of krill

A blue whale eats between 3,628.74 and 7,257.48 kg/4 and 8 tons – average 5,443.11 kg /6 tons – of krill a day.

And 4,920,000 golf balls have been sold around the world

820,000 are sold worldwide every day.

Fore!

WHILE YOU'RE ... HIKING ROUND YOSEMITE

It takes 6 to 7 days to hike the 96.6 km/60 miles of the Yosemite Grand Traverse in California.

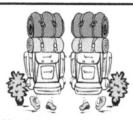

"Mine's heavier than yours."
"No, mine's heavier than yours."
"No, mine's heavier than yours."
"Remind me again why we're doing this."

A baby robin has eaten 2.13 m/7 ft of earthworms

Baby robins eat 4.27 m/14 ft of earthworms in two weeks.

And a Kingfisher chick has eaten 100 fish

With broods of eggs in April, July and possibly October, each Common Kingfisher chick is fed in rotation with 12 to 18 fish a day – 84 to 126 fish in 7 days.

Sperm whales have covered 6 times the

distance, over the largest volcano on Earth

Hiking over the 96.6 km/60 miles in 7 days is about 13.8 km/8.6 miles a day – about 1.7 km/1 mile an hour for an 8 hour day. Sperm whales swim at 10 km/h/6.2 mph – covering about 360 miles in the 7 days - above the 1,981.2 m/6,500 ft 'Tamu massif' volcano under the North Pacific waters of Japan. It's about as big as the British Isles or New Mexico. It's only 25% smaller than the Olympus Mons on Mars – so it's one of the largest in our solar system – but 98% larger than the largest active volcano of Hawaii's Mauna Loa. It was formed 130 to 145 million years ago.

Someone has climbed Kilimanjaro

It takes about 7 days to climb Kilimanjaro in Tanzania.

139

A balloon released into the jet stream has gone half way round the world

It takes two weeks for a balloon to travel round the world in the jet stream, at about 160 km/h/100 mph.

And it's half a day on the moon

The moon is tidally locked to the Earth and orbits us once every 4 weeks. A day there last 2 weeks, a night lasts 2 weeks, and a week is half of a day or night on the moon.

🕐 🕐 🕐 🕐 🕐 🕐 🕐

WHILE YOU'RE ... LEARNING TO PARAGLIDE

10 : days

It takes 10 days of instruction to basic certification for paragliding.

Companies that manufacture parachutes claim they work more than 99.9% of the time. So only 1 in a 1,000 of you needs to worry.

If at first you don't succeed, skydiving is not for you.

With a sudden upward gust of wind, Charlie found himself on a free flight to New York.

How Do You Compare – Speed-Wise?

The speed of paragliders is 20 to 75 km/h/12 to 47 mph, from stall speed to maximum speed.

So - at top speed (75 km/h/47 mph), it's an even race with a herd of wildebeest on an African plain (80.5 km/h/50 mph). Or a greyhound (74 km/h/46 mph).

But you'd lose against a Mexican Free-Tailed Bat, an Ostrich and a Swordfish (all 97 km/h/60 mph), and a horse-fly (140 km/h/90 mph).

You can easily beat an African Elephant (40 km/h/25 mph) and a crocodile (17 km/h/10.56 mph). And, in mid-range, you're about the same as a flying squirrel (32.93 km/h/20.46 mph).

A spam run has started and finished on your computer

Spam is regulated by different laws in different countries, and spammers must abide by the law of the country to
which they send Spam. The American Can-Spam (Controlling the Assault of Non-Solicited Pornography and Marketing) Act 2003, under which spammers have been sued for millions of dollars, includes that they must remove recipients from their list within 10 business days. The UK Act currently lacks any time restriction, allowing bombardment of UK computers indefinitely by spammers if they meet all other requirements.

Anything could taste different by the time you've finished

The average lifespan of a taste bud is 10 days; so some have been replaced. Your tongue has nearly 10,000 taste buds – Catfish have 100,000.

However far you paraglided - you can add 1,073,432 km/667,000 miles to it

The Earth travels through space at 107,343.25 km/h/66,700 mph. So you travelled 1,073,432.45 km/667,000 miles during the 10 days anyway.

"But meanwhile time flies; it flies never to be regained." *Virgil*

🕐 🕐 🕐 🕐 🕐 🕐 🕐 🕐

WHILE YOU'RE ... ON HOLIDAY

Legal entitlement (UK) is 28 days' annual paid holiday if you work five days a week. Employers can include bank holidays to make it a 5.6-week paid holiday a year.

1 : month

The average number of times that children ask 'Are we there yet?' on a week's vacation is 9.

They were delighted! The salesgirl said their swimming costumes were 'special' wool and wouldn't shrink in the sea.

141

On holiday, Brits eat a larder's-worth of 'home from home' comforts, and use 3 times more teabags than condoms.

Things Brits take on holiday: tomatoes, sardines, peanut butter, instant noodles, Marmite, a potato peeler, British coffee, biscuits and chocolate. 9 out of 10 don't use a third of the clothes they pack; and they take about a third the number of condoms as teabags. But they're reluctant to give up their hols, even if budgeting.

If you don't have your own set of wheels, Lima in Peru's the best bet for getting a taxi – with odds in your favour of more than 200,000 to 1.

Lima has over 210,000 taxis; Mexico City – 108,000 registered cabs; and London – 23,000 black taxi cabs. The average speed of a taxi cab is 17.7 km/h/11 mph.

You'll use a vending machine 9 times

We use one 115 times a year – 2.2 times a week and 8.8 times in the month. 13 people a year are killed in America by vending machines falling on them.

> **Motto: Change is inevitable except from vending machines.**

In 1983, a Californian decided the best rays for his tan were at 6,000 feet. Ingeniously, he tied 42 helium balloons to his deckchair and secured that by a long rope to the earth. Settled in and bronzing his body up high, he was jolted into the realisation that his deckchair rope had snapped and he, his balloons and his deckchair floated up to 15,000 feet. To enhance his adventure, he passed an aeroplane, with the pilot reporting him as a UFO. Luckily, he had an air pistol. He floated back to earth, shooting each balloon in turn but with his deckchair having a mind of its own. That hit a power cable, blacking out an area of California, which, he decided, was an inevitable end to the day as he stumbled home in the dark.

Americans eat 3.6 kg/8 lbs of ice each, and buy 4 million kites between them

An average American eats 0.9 kg/2 lbs of ice a week, and 50 million kites are sold in the States every year – making 3,846,153 sold in the 4 weeks.

142

Your heart beats nearly 3 million times

The average person's heart beats 101,000 times a day – 36,865,000 times a year – that's 2,828,000 times while you're hopefully relaxing and de-stressing it on a 28 day holiday.

1 in 6 of us comes back from holiday feeling like we need a holiday.

We also 'lift' towels (first choice) and the remote batteries (second choice) from the hotel.

Woman: "Now you've recovered from the overnight flight, the five hours of customs, the 2 day bus ride, the plane hopping, and the tummy upset, we'll have a lovely holiday for two days."

Over 90,000 people visit London Zoo

With 1.1 million yearly visitors to the zoo, that's 91,666.67 a month. The zoo has 20,166 animals and 698 species (2023). It's active in conservation projects in over 50 countries worldwide.

2.1 billion people visit YouTube worldwide

That's the number of users who visit it each month. The first YouTube video, on 23rd April 2005, was 'Me at the zoo' by co-founder, Jawed Karim. That 18 second film has been viewed over 227 million times.

A nurse was called to tend to a most unfortunate holidaymaker. He'd been stung by a jellyfish and, in agony, had taken refuge in a beach hut – where he was hit on the head when a plank of wood fell from the roof. The nurse listened sympathetically and got up to close the door of his room to treat him, unfortunately slamming it a little too hard – so that the ceiling collapsed onto the bed in which he was lying.

"The camper van's ready. We'll be in Peru by the time the kids find out we've gone."

Playing for Time
Technology

"I don't know what I did, but I seem to be able to watch YouTube videos on the microwave."

Playing for Time
Technology

Sending or reading a single text can distract a driver for just under 5 seconds (4.6 seconds) (the Virginia Tech Transportation Institute).

Is what you have
to tell someone
more important
than your life?

"If you hadn't texted me to meet you here, I wouldn't have read it while I was driving to meet you here."

After four bottles of wine, the Wesselhampton Ladies Yoga Club had to pretend to drive home. It was Linda's turn to hold the steering wheel this time.

Seven out of a hundred people are drunk, and one may be in your line of traffic

It's estimated that, at any one time, including during the 5 seconds of sending or reading a text, 7% of the world's population is drunk.

1 in 3 of us loses control of the car when we sneeze

33% of drivers have lost control of their vehicle for up to 5 seconds when their eyes close automatically when they sneeze. 7% of drivers report causing a road accident due to sneezing. And there's 2,500 accidents a week in the UK by those with cold and flu symptoms in the winter.

145

"Atchooooo!"

You could be following one of the 3 in 10 who fall asleep at the wheel for those 5 seconds

Data from Australia, England, Finland, and other European nations, is that drowsy driving causes 10 to 30 % of all crashes. In America, the main cause of sleep deprivation is addiction to using tech devices late into the night.

And news just in … to the driver dozing at the lights on 5th and Main - WAKE UP!!! You're blocking a Star Trek Convention coach and they've set phasers to stun.

At 96.5 km/h/60 mph, looking only at your cell phone, you've gone 13 car lengths more than your stopping distance, into an accident

Travelling at 96.5 km/h/60 mph – 26.8 m/88 ft a second - you've travelled 134.11 m/440 ft in the 5 seconds. The Thinking Distance for stopping at 96.5 km/h/60 mph is 18 m/59 ft, and the Braking Distance is 55 m/180.45 ft – totalling 73 m/239.45 ft. So you've travelled 61.11 m/ 200.5 ft further than the distance in which you should have stopped. The length of the average car is 4.5 m/14.8 ft, so you've travelled about

"I think it's easier if you point to the bits of you that *don't* hurt!"

13.5 car lengths more than the distance in which you should have stopped.

⏰ ⏰ ⏰ ⏰ ⏰ ⏰ ⏰ ⏰

WHILE YOU'RE ... TEXTING

Writing a text message takes an average of 45 seconds.

45 : seconds

💬 You're ... 💬
1 of 5 billion using texts, and you spend 23 hours a week texting.
Dissatisfied with your relationship the more you text your partner.
More likely to get the truth in a text than in a phone conversation.
A study by Cornell University, New York, found that 37% of students tell lies in their phone conversations. People are more truthful in face to face conversations and in anything written - including text messaging.

Phil converted the organ keys to QWERTY and hooked up his cell phone. On a good day, he used all his text allowance and played Bach's Toccata.

It's another 'Day in the Life' while you're writing a text

The Beatles' song 'A Day in the Life' ends with a note held for 40 seconds – about the time it takes to write a text message.

If you're still talking about what you did yesterday, you haven't done much today.

The Sun's moved through 11,225km/6,975 miles

The Sun travels at 250 km/155 miles a second. And, just as the planets in our solar system orbit the sun over one year, it takes one cosmic year for our entire solar system (sun, planets, moon, asteroids and comets) to orbit the centre of the Milky Way galaxy at 800,000 kph/500,000 mph. So in 90 seconds – the time of two texts – we all move 20,000 km/12,500 miles in our orbit around the centre of the galaxy, with the sun taking 225-250 million years to complete this journey.

Your body's made 90 million red blood cells

The human body destroys and makes about two million new red blood cells every second – making 90 million while you wrote a text.

Mobsters are having a pager buried with them in case family members want to message them in the afterlife. Graves in Sicily have been heard to beep.

In the time of two texts, you could have decided if you fancy someone, if you were face to face

It takes 90 seconds to 4 minutes to know. And it's not much about what they're saying (only 7%), but 55% body language, and 38% tone and speed of voice. Staring into each other's eyes is a very powerful attraction.

And you could give someone 15 hugs in the time of one text - and get some 'love drug' from half of them

An average hug lasts 3 seconds. A longer 20 second embrace releases oxytocin – 'the love drug'. It's produced daily in our blood and brains, and hugging is one of the fastest ways to get an 'oxy-fix'. It's a nerve calmer, and it reduces blood pressure and the stress hormone, cortisol, improving sleep.

147

WHILE YOU'RE ... KEPT ON HOLD BY A CALL CENTRE

6.8 : minutes

The average waiting time in a call centre for USA Social Services is 6 minutes 48 seconds. We spend an estimated 60 hours a year or 1.15 hours a week listening to 'muzak'. 85% of consumers, waiting for customer support on the phone, have yelled and sworn (USA Today).

Nearly 320 people have bought or received a Bible around the world

Your call is important to us. You now have 16 options to choose from ...

Every minute, 47 Bibles are sold or distributed throughout the world – 319.6 in 6.8 minutes.

"... So I said to Jim 'if you think I'm that kind of a girl' ... and he said ... ."

The Bible is the most shop-lifted book in the USA.
The Old Testament is written using a vocabulary of about 5,800 words; the New Testament – about 4,800 words. Today's newspapers use about 6,000 words.

Over 1.15 billion litres/250 million gallons of water has tumbled over the edge of Niagara and Angel Falls
Niagara Falls isn't as high as the Angel Falls but it's much wider. So they both pour about the same amount of water over their edges – about 2,832,000 litres/620,000 gallons a second.

Someone in the world is singing, or humming, 'Hey Jude'. And with the 6.8-minute call centre wait, you should be talking to someone before they finish the 'Nah-nah-nah-nanana-nah's'
'Hey Jude' is the most popular Beatle's song on both YouTube and i-Tunes. It's 7.04 minutes on YouTube – longer than you should be kept on an average 6.8 minute call centre hold.

Take a sad song and make it better

Your video should be at least 10 minutes. That's 1,024 MB and, with a high-speed connection, the upload is 1 to 5 minutes per MB – averaging 2.5 minutes a MB. So, it's 40 minutes for a 1,024 MB at 2.5 minutes a MB and, with converting time, averages an hour. 3.7 million new videos are uploaded to YouTube a day.

We've come from:
1895: the first practical radio invented by Marconi - to ...
2005: 14th February - YouTube was founded on the Internet

HELLO WORLD

Your potential YouTube audience for that hour was over 208 million

2.1 billion of the world's 4.95 billion online population use YouTube. They watch 5 billion videos daily, which works out as 208,333,333 videos watched in each hour of a 24 hour day - with an average 19.35 minute viewing session, and 70% using mobiles. 30,000 hours of content is uploaded every hour. YouTube was originally intended as a dating site for digital personal ads.

"Look! We're on YouTube!" he yelled. **"Wave at the camera and smile."**
"Is that before or after I lose my lunch?" she screamed.

Listening to its own hour-long CD – or your music – your pet cat could be hearing sounds that you can't hear

There are CDs made especially for cats. They can hear ultrasound (levels from 20,000 Hz up to several gigahertz) above our normal hearing range of 20 Hz to 20,000 Hz. Pigeons can also hear ultrasound, and other animals that can hear sounds that we can't, are the Katydid (sounds up to 4-5,000 vibrations a second), bats (hearing prey walking on sand) and elephants (14 and 35 Hz – sounds too low for us to hear).

149

The bacteria in your ears have increased 700-fold from wearing headphones

Wearing headphones for an hour increases the bacteria in your ear by 700 times.

 And if you're a guy using a laptop, the temperature of your testicles has risen enough to affect your sperm count

A PC on a man's lap can raise the temperature of his testicles about 6 degrees in an hour. It's just a 2 degree rise level that's enough to reduce sperm count.

ⓖ ⓖ ⓖ ⓖ ⓖ ⓖ ⓖ ⓖ

WHILE YOU'RE ... GIVING UP SEX FOR THE INTERNET

2 : weeks

An Intel survey found nearly half of women (46%) would forfeit sex rather than give up the Internet for two weeks.

I'm not addicted to Facebook. I just check it when I have time ... coffee time, lunch time, teatime, bed time, this time, that time ... anytime.

His reckless moment ...

"But the computer's just there and my bid's coming up," she said.

Claude's Calamity of a Choral Constable

"What's the ticket for?"
"Your horn's slightly off-key."
"But what about him jay walking?!"

2 out of 3 of you will irritably honk your car horn at least twice

Two-thirds of drivers honk their car horn at least once a week. Most cars honk in the key of F.

150

In the two weeks, you'll spend nearly a day and a half on social networking sites – and 16 hours checking emails, 14 hours on Facebook and 9 hours on YouTube

In a week, users average nearly 2.5 hours a day on social networking sites – 17.5 hours a week and 35 hours in two weeks - and 7 hours a week on Facebook and over 4.5 hours on YouTube. We also spend 8 hours a week checking emails.

Celia labelled her cat photo "Fluffy', and social networking was born.

How skinny would I get if I had to pedal to keep the computer on?

Brits On-Line

Half of us know our on-line friends are superficial. A quarter of us:

- lie or exaggerate about who we've met and what we've done
- are lonely
- are more confident on-line and of making friends in cyberspace than the real world
- prefer contact at a distance – text or on-line chats rather than phoning or meeting someone

A third of us have more 'cyber friends' (even if they're really strangers) and communicate with them more than we do with our fewer human friends.

You'll argue with your partner six times in bed, and apologise ten times

Tessa felt bad at being on the Internet so much so she sent her husband a Facebook message.

Married couples disagree in bed about 160 times a year – an average of just over 3 times a week. 1 in 5 will argue about who should get up to check the doors, at bedtime. And we apologize 5 times a week.

Darling - meet me in the bedroom at 9 o'clock?

xxx

151

She'll check her horoscope six times
Women check their horoscopes 3 times a week.

"OMG. I forgot to check where Jupiter is in my stars."

Miss 'Rita Thunderbird' had a spectacular act of being shot out of a cannon. Sadly, more than once, she remained firmly stuck in the cannon after the gunpowder was lit, And on one occasion – at Battersea in 1977 - she was ready in her gold lame bikini, the gunpowder was lit and she, again, remained cosily stuck in her cannon – while her bra was shot across the River Thames.

He'll claim his couple of tipples a day are just for his marathon training
The average number of alcoholic drinks that male marathon runners have is two a day – twenty-eight in two weeks.

Did someone say-
"Bite Me?"

"Here's to exercise! Cheers!"

And a third of you will watch five scary movies
A third watch a scary movie or TV show 5 times in two weeks.

WHILE YOU'RE ... PLAYING SOLITAIRE

17 million : years

It's estimated that throughout the world, in a year, we spend up to 150 billion hours – the equivalent of 17 million years – of human effort playing computer games like Solitaire.

"Life is a game – play it."
Mother Teresa

After bunking off work for two days, Jeff had finally beaten his fastest time to win at Solitaire.

Going back the same time frame, the Colorado Plateau of the Grand Canyon was forming, and humans and chimps were going their own evolutionary ways

Between 17 and 5 million years ago, pressures from North American and Pacific plates formed the Colorado Plateau. And the Miocene geological epoch (23 to 2.5 million years ago) included the evolution of humans and their separation from apes, alongside a natural world of deer, snakes, turtles, camels, whales and dolphins, and giant crocodiles, huge sharks, and birds with a 762cms/25 foot wingspan. Continents were forming into those we know - with grasslands and a warm climate.

And now the same human effort, that we all put into playing computer games in a year, could get us over half way to our nearest star, going by car at 160 km/h/100 mph

It would take a car, travelling at 160 km/h/100 mph, about 30 million years to reach our nearest star, Proxima Centauri (4.2 light years away).

"I've printed the Google map ... really simple. Head for Mars and bear left."

There are more stars in the universe than there are grains of sand on all the beaches in the world, but only about 3,000 stars are visible to the naked eye. If you counted the stars in just one galaxy at a rate of one every second, it would take about 3,000 years. That's twice as long as it took the 40 authors to write the Bible – 1,500 years – before it was also translated into Klingon, the Star Trek language, just in case we do go by car to the nearest star. By the way, the USS Enterprise spacecraft travels a little faster – at maximum warp speed it's 1,129,355,149.390 kph/701,748,755.636 mph.

Right Place, Right Time
Travel

"Please keep all your belongings
with you at all times."

Right Place, Right Time
Travel

WHILE YOU'RE ...
CHANGING A BIKE TYRE

5 : minutes

The average time is 5 minutes.

> My biggest fear is that, when I die, my wife will sell my bicycles for what I told her they cost.

By the time you've changed it, your dog's forgotten why you stopped

I ride bikes to meet women ... nurses, mostly.

As the bee said to the rose ...

"Hiya, Bud!"

A dog's memory lasts between 2 and 5 minutes (University of Michigan).

And a nearby bee has flapped its wings 55,000 times

To stay in the air, bees flap their wings about 11,000 times a minute. That's what causes the 'buzz'.

WHILE YOU'RE ... WAITING FOR A BUS

6 : minutes

The average time: 6 minutes (Passenger Wait Time Perceptions at Bus Stops – Ohio State University, Chicago, Illinois).

The guy at the front is the driver – not Quasimodo. So only ring the bell once.

12 lawsuits have been started in America
There's one in the USA every 30 seconds.

Lawyer 1: "When he went, had you gone and had she, if she wanted to and were able, for the time being excluding all the restraints on her not to go, gone also, would he have brought you, meaning you and she, with him to the station?"

Lawyer 2: "Objection. That question should be taken out and shot."

684 new cars have been made in the world

The car was invented by Karl Benz in 1885. Each year, 60 million cars are made worldwide. That's 164,383.56 new cars every day, and 6,849.32 an hour, 114.16 a minute, and 1.9 a second.

You could lose 30 calories using a hula hoop in the 6 minute wait

Your Car
- is one in a billion – the number on the world's roads
- may be the 1 out of 4 made in China
- could be red – the most popular colour worldwide

Hula hooping burns 3 to 7 calories a minute – averaging 5 calories a minute. Depending on the style and type of hoop and your metabolism, weight and body composition, it can also trim your waist. The record of 243 revolutions of a hula hoop in one minute was by Gregory Sean Dillon (USA) in California, on 20 March 2012.

WHILE YOU'RE ... ON THE LONDON UNDERGROUND

15 : minutes

Westminster to Piccadilly Circus on the London Tube is about 15 minutes.

They took busking on the platforms to a new level.

156

Someone's milked a cow by hand

It's about 15 minutes to milk a cow, and she can produce 40 glasses of milk a day.

The average lifespan of a dairy cow is 15 years, and the most played song on American radio in the 20th Century was 'You've Lost that Loving Feeling' – a colossal 45 years of continuous play if the 8 million times were put back to back. So, if the song has been continuously played in the cow shed, it would have been heard by the grandmother and the mother of your current cow on its 15th birthday.

Women in Brisbane and Paris have each started labour

Regular contractions of 15 minute intervals can herald the start of labour. The baby in Brisbane, Australia will always celebrate his or her birthday eight hours ahead of the one in Paris, France, if both remain in the same place.

Black and white are in unison in the Universe – spinning 269,813,212,200 km/ 167,654,157,300 miles in 15 minutes

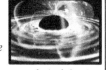

Astronomers have found that the spin of a super-massive black hole is, at its surface, almost the speed of white light - 299,792,458 metres a second/186,282.397 miles a second. And they've seen a gas cloud, larger than our Solar System, destroyed by a black hole at the galactic core. A super-massive black hole is thought to be at the centre of nearly all galaxies, including our Milky Way.

And someone's getting 6 hours sleep, meditating

Meditation can provide deeper rest than that gained by sleep; and 15 minutes of meditation can equal 6 hours of sleep.

Benefits of Meditation
Scientific studies have shown that even just 15 minutes of meditation increases our focus and attention, creativity, empathy, memory, absorption of new information, productivity, intelligence and brain power– all leading to more positive emotions.

Jo was so enthralled with his meditation book that he passed straight to total relaxation before he finished the Contents page.

WHILE YOU'RE ... ON AUTO MAINTENANCE

It's approximately 20 minutes to change a flat tyre and 20 minutes to change the oil in a regular family car.

30% OF WOMEN AND 4% OF MEN DON'T KNOW HOW TO CHANGE A FLAT TYRE

"It's just the oil sump," he said. "Lucky I swerved round that bull in the road." "Yes, Darling. But you know you said you wouldn't like to meet it again ... "

Car breakdowns are one of the reasons for traffic holdups. Others are accidents, road construction and repairs, and harsh weather conditions.

When 89-year-old Mae West was starring in 'Sextette', she couldn't keep pace with script changes. The director, Ken Hughes, devised what he thought was a good plan and had a small radio receiver concealed in her wig. The idea was for Mr Hughes to whisper her lines to Ms West just before she was due to deliver them. However, this was not the best of plans. Firstly, the other actors were more than a bit put off when they kept hearing Mr Hughes' voice coming from the wig with the answers to lines they were just about to, but hadn't yet, delivered. Then – by some fluke, the wig wavelength picked up that of a police helicopter. And everyone on set froze when, during a passionate love scene, Ms West spoke those unforgettable words: 'Traffic on the Hollywood Freeway is bogged down'.

You could be playing three hands of Bridge

Duplicate bridge is the most widely used form of the card game for club and tournament play. It allows 7-8 minutes per hand with 22 to 26 hands each session. The same arrangement of the 52 cards into the four hands is played at each table.

Or travel faster by ostrich – covering 24 km/15 miles

The ostrich is the fastest animal on two legs. It can sprint for 30 minutes at up to 72 km/h/45 mph – at which speed it covers 24 km/15 miles in 20 minutes - and with a peak of 97 km/h/60 mph for short periods, and strides of 3.7 m/12 ft.

158

WHILE YOU'RE ... HAVING A DRIVING LESSON

1.5 : hours

A driving lesson takes one or two hours – average 1.5 hours.

The average for learning to drive is 45 hours of professional tuition and 20 hours of private practise.

Men drivers get most speeding tickets – 63%.

"Really, Mr Jones. I don't know why you keep turning left when it makes me slide over and press right up against you, like this."

Car Accident Report: I pulled away from the side of the road, glanced at my mother-in-law, and headed over the embankment.

"You're right! Susie *has* broken her record. She's managed to park over four spaces this time ...."

Women take 20 seconds longer than men to parallel park; and 40% of them break out in a sweat before doing it.

In the Scottish Glencoe Wood, a deer is half way through its daily sleep

A roe deer, a donkey and a horse all sleep for 3 hours a day.

Dear Deer ...

In Sweden – 20% of road accidents involve an elk
In Canada – 1 in 300 involves a moose
In Scotland – 7,000 a year involve a deer
In UK – 74,000 a year are collisions with a deer
In USA – 1.5 million a year involve a deer

AIRPORT

ARRIVALS

For some reason, nobody objected to Darth Vader jumping to the front of the taxi line.

London cabbies are ferrying 300,000 passengers round the capital

There are an estimated 200,000 cab rides in London in an hour.

Knowledge is realizing that the street is one way; wisdom is looking both directions anyway.

Someone's recharging their electric car

A 22kW fast-charging point, in public spaces, work places, and shopping car parks, can fully charge a car battery in 1 to 2 hours.

Man: "Darling, my new electric car might run out of charge."
Woman: "Well, it'll make a change from running out of petrol."

You know you're on the right track when you become uninterested in looking back.

And police are driving on sirens at breakneck speed on emergency calls in Rome, Moscow, Wellington and Beijing

Most cities and towns around the world have 24 hour police cover. Car chases have been known to last 1.5 hours.

In 1969, Mrs Beatrice Park took her fifth diving test and having confused the accelerator with the clutch, drove into the River Wey in Guildford, England. She and her driving tester climbed onto the roof of the car. When they were rescued, the examiner was in a state of shock, cradling his clipboard. When Mrs Park asked if she'd passed her test, the rescue service could only reply: 'We cannot say until we have seen the examiner's report'.

Check-in time for a European flight is at least 2 hours before departure. For International flights - 3 hours before departure, and for domestic flights within the same country – 1.5 hours.

Know where you're going and
how you're going to get there.
If not - you'll end up
somewhere else.

Waiting for the plane, they
got bored building houses
with playing cards, so they
started using the coffee cups.

20 million Mexican free-tailed bats

**may have already
taken to the air in
Texas, and eaten 41.7
tons of insects**

The colony of 20 million Mexican free-tailed bats of Bracken Cave, near San Antonio in Texas, eats 250 tons of insects every night – that's 41.7 tons in 2 hours, assuming a 12 hour night. Bats make up a quarter of all mammal species; and they always turn left when leaving a cave.

Airport Waiting Games

1 Tip out a whole box of matches. Ask your friends to make a square, moving only two of the matches.
2 Write the words 'Up yours, Blinky-Bop' on a piece of paper. Ask your friends to write a love poem of four lines, including the words.
3 Write down the entire alphabet. Ask your friends to write down the hidden word.
4 Find a picture of an earthworm. Ask your friends to write, in 50 words, the role of the earthworm in our galaxy.
5 Write the words 'The End' on a piece of paper. Ask your friends which film you're thinking about.

9,000 people at the airport have seen James Bond in action

Half the world's population has seen at least one James Bond movie. Taking Heathrow as an average for a large airport, there are normally about 9,000 people passing through Heathrow in an hour – which is half of your 2 hour check-in waiting time. So 18,000 pass through Heathrow in 2 hours – and half of that population has seen James Bond doing his bit - or every other person you see at the airport and on the plane has seen at least one James Bond movie.

*James ...
oh, James...*

161

You could be learning to scuba dive in Bermuda

Lessons are just over 2 hours long.

The Bermuda Pyramids

There are huge glass pyramids 2,000 m/1.24 miles below Bermuda on the sea bed - three times larger than those of Cheops in Egypt. Pyramids are natural generators of power, and some of those around the world have discharged beams of energy into space. There have been discoveries of scattered 'ruins' in the coastal waters off the Florida Keys, the Bahamas, and Cuba – including in the 'Bermuda Triangle' - suggesting a large ancient civilization.

Or you could be on an organized picnic in Centennial Park, Atlanta, or Regents Park, London, or the Hanging Gardens in Mumbai

An officially-run event is usually 2 hours. The Guinness World Record for the most people at a picnic was 22,232 in Lisbon, Portugal on 20th June 2009.

It was the day they all agreed they'd leave their camera phones at home ...

If you never go, you'll never know.

162

WHILE YOU'RE ... CRUISING ACROSS THE ATLANTIC

1 : week

The Queen Mary Transatlantic Crossing from New York to Southampton takes 7 days.

O billows bounding far,
How wet how wet ye are!
When first my gaze ye met,
I said 'Those waves are wet'.
A E Houseman

The Sat Nav said this was the best place to wave off Auntie June on her once-in-a-lifetime cruise.

More than 75,000 people have visited the Statue of Liberty

About 4 million visit the Statue each year. It was dedicated on 28th October 1886 and built in the style of an ancient Grecian representing the birthplace of democracy. The seven rays in her crown represent the seven continents and seven seas; her tablet is dated July 4th 1776 (the 'birth' of America). Her torch represents her full name – 'Liberty Enlightening the World', with the broken chains of tyranny at her feet.

A key to lock the door up. A bag to hold your clothes. A ticket for the journey. To where the sea breeze blows.

You could be accompanied for half the time ... by Humpback Whales all singing in rhyme

The whales are capable of speeds of 48% of that of the Queen Mary. Their cruising speed is 14.5 km/h/9 mph but they can travel at 27 km/h/17 mph - versus the 30 knots or 56 km/h/35 mph of the Queen Mary. The whales could therefore cover 2,816 km/1,750 miles of the 5,632 km/3,500 mile journey. Research shows that the song of whales is in rhymes, and that over 35% of the songs of the Humpback Whale contain rhyming sounds. The rhyme-like structures are most likely to be in songs containing the most material to be remembered by the whales.

163

It helps make up for half your yearly lost sleep

We lose the equivalent of 15 days sleep each year, just lying awake and fretting. Leave your troubles behind for a week.

A professional ballerina has danced her way through a dozen pairs of shoes

... the number they can get through every week.

Woman in hat: "Yesterday it was a swimsuit. She wears less every day."
Man: "Yea! Can't wait for tomorrow!"

And on the world's roads, over 950,000 cars have been added to the traffic

Every year, about 50 million cars (old and new) are added to the world's roads – 961,538 a week.

❂ ❂ ❂ ❂ ❂ ❂ ❂ ❂

WHILE YOU'RE ... FLYING TO THE MOON

26 : days

If a 747 plane could fly to the Moon, at its normal speed of 643.7 km/h/400 mph, it would take it 625 hours – 26 days – to make the 402,336 km/250,000 mile journey.

A computer hard drive now has more capacity than NASA had available to use in its first rockets to the Moon.

The Moon is a million times dryer than the Gobi Desert. It's 27% the size of the Earth; and the full moon always rises at sunset and sets at sunrise.

164

In the North Pacific Ocean, an octopus has eaten 11.7 kg/25.74 lbs of shrimp, crab, clams and fish

An average weight of a Giant Pacific Octopus is 15 kg/33 lbs. It eats 2 to 4% of its body weight daily. Taking an average of 3% of its body weight, it eats 0.45 kg/0.99 lbs daily, and 11.7 kg/25.74 lbs in 26 days.

The planet Mercury's completed about a third of its orbit, 152.08 million km/94.5 million miles away

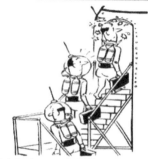

Mercury orbits the Sun within the Earth's orbit at 28°. It's the smallest and closet planet to the Sun in the Solar System. It takes 88 days for it to orbit the Sun – the shortest orbit of all the Solar System planets. It's named after the Roman god Mercurius, who was the messenger of the gods.

3rd Astronaut: "Oh, great! Now we'll have to go to Mercury via 24 Acacia Avenue to pick up his spare helmet."

While, in the Indian Ocean, a school of anchovy is darting 350 km/218 miles over the Rodinia 'lost' supercontinent – the billion year old 'Motherland' of ancient Earth

The common length of an Indian anchovy is 12 cm and, swimming an average of 1.3 body lengths per second, that's 0.56 km/h/0.35 mph and 349.44 km/218.4 miles in 26 days. Scientists have found fragments of Rodinia, an ancient 'lost' supercontinent, beneath the floor of the Indian Ocean. Rodinia contained most of Earth's single large landmass, and existed between 1.1 billion and 750 million years ago.

And the Moon's nearly completed one orbit of the Earth

The Moon orbits the Earth every 27.32 days.

Oh, hey there!

What's up, friend?

Don't tell us the sky's the limit when there are footsteps on the Moon.

WHILE YOU'RE ... DRIVING ROUTE 66

1 : month

With stopping for sight-seeing, it takes about a month to drive the 3,665 km/2,278 miles of Route 66 from Chicago to Santa Monica, California.

Those that say 'you can't take it with you' never saw a car packed for a vacation trip.

Established on November 11th 1926, Route 66 was one of the original roads of the US Highway System. It's also known as the Will Rogers Highway or the Main Street of America or the Mother Road. Since June 27th 1985, most of it has been replaced and the original is called 'Historic Route 66', using new roads to cover the direction of the old Route 66. It covers 8 states and crosses 3 time zones (Central Time – Illinois, Missouri, Kansas, Oklahoma and Texas; Mountain Time – New Mexico and Arizona; and Pacific Time in California).

Under the Atlantic Ocean, two huge plates of the Earth's surface are growing apart by 2.54 mm/0.1 inch

The African and American plates are moving apart about 2.54 mm/0.1 inch a month. That's about the same rate as fingernails grow.

States-Side Smiles

Kansas: Police fired two rifle shots at an alligator in a garden, before realising it was a concrete garden ornament.

Texas: A demolition company pulled down a perfectly stable house, instead of one damaged by a tornado, a block away.

California: A policeman was fined a month's pay for harassment – for giving his mother-in-law 43 traffic tickets.

If you do the trip with your partner, 1 in 6 of you will argue, and up to 196 times, including about speeding and parking

16% of couples, who've taken a road trip together, reckon it damaged their relationship temporarily. A survey found that couples row 7 times a day. In a year they argue about 'driving too fast' (91 times) and 'parking the car' (77 times). Those two

"Your wife said it was the lorry's fault for parking where she wanted to. And that she's very upset you shouted at her."

issues are 14 of 196 arguments in the month on the road with your partner.

 You're twice as likely to shake hands with a man than a woman – 24 times compared to 12 times
In one study, men shake hands 6 times a week and women – 3 times a week.

And you're best not to ask a woman the way

On average, a woman tells a lie about 700 times a year – making 13.46 times a week and 53.8 times while you're on the road. But asking a man for directions might be a problem - see Page 98. Men have trouble asking for directions, so what are your chances of them giving you any?!

…would I lie to you?

Top Tips for Lies
If a woman says she's 'fine' – it means:
Feelings Inside Not Expressed - or
Feeling Inadequate Needing Encouragement.
If a guy says 'I'll never lie to you' – or
'I already did that, Honey' – they're the top 'man lies'.

"I don't know where we are, but this road's an adventure to somewhere."

167

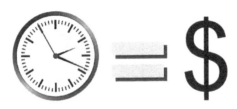

Investing Time

Work

"I like to spend my journey to work reading fiction."

Investing Time
Work

WHILE YOU'RE ... READING A LETTER

1 : minute

We read at 180 to 220 words a minute, the rate at which we speak.
A one-page A4 letter has about 220 to 250 words.

A computer user near to you has blinked 7 times

We blink 16 to 20 times a minute – but only 7 times a minute when using computer screens.

"You wanted this letter urgently, didn't you?"

Your blood has been all round your body once

Blood travels at 91 cms/3 ft a second when it leaves the heart, slowing down as it gets into smaller arteries and capillaries. It takes 45 seconds to a minute to travel around the body.

For 7 out of 10 drivers passing by you, duetting with their car radio – it's the Bee Gees

A Seat survey found that 20% of men enjoyed singing along to Take That, Shirley Bassey or Wham! when alone in their car. For all drivers, Westlife were 12%, Abba was 25%, and the outright joint winners at 71% were the Bee Gees and the Scissor Sisters. Redheads sing in their cars more than anyone else.

And 24,000 objects are whizzing around Earth's orbit above you

Every minute of every day, over 24,500 objects, of 10 cm/ 3.9 inches or more in diameter, orbit the Earth at up to 40,233.6 km/h/25,000 mph (Space Surveillance Network) of which only 560 of them are operational satellites. The rest is space debris - defunct satellites, launch vehicles and rocket stages.

WHILE YOU'RE ... ON A COFFEE BREAK

15 : minutes

The average time for a coffee break at work is 15 minutes.

Miss Jones – I see you bought the industrial size coffee machine!

In Italy, women are preparing three-quarters of their meals for the day

Italian women prepare food for an average of 20 minutes a day, and watch TV cookery programmes for 4 hours a week. UK women spend 8 hours a week (18 days a year) in the kitchen, including 20 minutes a day (2 hours 20 minutes a week) relaxing with the TV or a paper, and a cup of tea or coffee – or with friends.

In Canada, someone's skiing 6 km/3.7 miles down Whistler Mountain

Whistler is a ski resort 125 km/77.7 miles north of Vancouver, Canada. It was one of the venues for the 21st Winter Olympics in February 2010. The regular speed of a skier is 16 to 32 km/h/10 to 20 mph – averaging 24 km/h/15 mph.

In the Sozh River of Belarus, a beaver is holding its breath the whole time

Beavers can remain underwater for 15 minutes without surfacing. They're the second largest rodent after the capybara.

A grey sky turned blue somewhere in the world

Clouds move at wind speed – an average of 48 to 64 kph/30 to 40 mph at 3,048 to 4,572 m/10,000 to 15,000 feet. Sunlight is scattered by gases and particles in the air when it reaches Earth's atmosphere. Blue light is scattered the most because it travels as shorter, smaller waves – making the sky blue. So, assuming clouds are moving at 48 kph/30 mph, in 15 minutes the clouds have moved 7.5 miles to reveal a hint of the blue sky.

"Coffee and love are best when they're hot."
German Proverb

170

And you could catch a few minutes kip
Your initial light sleeping pattern is for 5 to 10 minutes. So, in your 15 minute coffee break, you could be zonked into some of the 10 to 25 minutes of 'true sleep'.

🕐 🕐 🕐 🕐 🕐 🕐 🕐

WHILE YOU'RE ...
DEALING WITH SPAM

29 : minutes

In an 8-hour working day, 29 minutes are spent dealing with uninvited communications, including spam, and unwanted calls and emails.

1.45 billion spam emails are sent a day worldwide - 45% of global emailing activity. The USA generated the most spam (25.35%); and Russia (19.84%). Pharmacy products are 45% of spam. *So why do spam?* – Profit. Research found that, even with a response rate of 0.0023%, sales were US $1,500/£1,206 with £1,150/£925 profit. Spam costs businesses about $20.5 billion/£16.4 billion worldwide. According to Nucleus Research, the average loss per employee is about $1,934/£1,551.2 a year, with decreased productivity and technical expenses incurred by the company due to spam.

"I shouldn't read spam. Claim for an accident! Enlarge your you-know-what! I walked into a car while I was looking down at my you-know-what."

Email spam is junk mail sent in bulk. The name started in the 1990s and comes from a Monty Python sketch in which Spam luncheon meat was portrayed as being unavoidable and repetitive, and the name is now used for unsolicited and unwanted emails.

You
could be enjoying 6.4 km/4 miles of San Francisco by cable car instead
The speed of a San Francisco cable car is determined by the speed of the cable they grip and release to stop. In San Francisco, the cable speed is 15.29 km/h/9.5 mph. The San Francisco cable cars are the only mobile national monuments in America.

171

4,176 people worldwide have moved home

Globally, in one minute, 144 people move to a new home.

7,656 babies have been born and 3,306 people have died worldwide

There are 4.4 births and 1.9 deaths in the world every second.

It is estimated that 117 billion humans have existed on Earth (Population Reference Bureau). Our global population (2023) is about 8 billion. So, those of us currently alive are about 7% of the total number of humans who have ever lived on Earth.

And ...

Each one of us is 'worth every cent'

Our body has up to 40 trillion cells, and there's $40 trillion in liquid assets in circulation in the world — coins, notes, bills, and money in savings and check accounts. So every one of us is 'worth every cent'.

Over 750,000 zippers have been made

About 14 billion zippers are produced a year. That's 38,356,164.4 a day, 1,598,173.5 an hour, and 26,636.2 a minute. In the 29 minutes, 772,449.8 have been made. Zippers are also called 'slide fasteners'.

The moon has moved 1,780 kilometres/ 1,106miles

The moon orbits Earth at 3,683 kmph/2,288.5 mph. That's 61.38 kilometres per minute/38.14 miles per minute, and 1,780.02 kilometres/1,106.06 miles in the 29 minutes you're dealing with spam.

You could match the world crocheting record

In 30 minutes, Lisa Gentry of Monroe, Louisiana, USA managed 5,118 crochet stitches – 170.6 stitches a minute - to establish a record of being the fastest crocheter in the world. That's 4,947.4 stitches in 29 minutes.

435 cans of Spam have been opened around the world

A can of Spam luncheon meat is opened every four seconds.

There's a Spam museum at Austin, Minnesota, USA – nicknamed 'The Guggenham' or 'Porkopolis'. The gift shop has Spam Bigfoot postcards, Spam mouse pads, infant hoodies, the Sir Can-A-Lot character, Spam Fan licence plates, Spam golf tees as well as Spam hats and mugs. Spam was first introduced in 1937. It was a 1940's icon and sustained many through WWII.

A bee's flown nearly 12 km/7.5 miles using maths calculations faster and more efficiently than your computer can do them (The American Naturalist)

Bees fly at an average of 24 km/h/14.9 mph – 0.4 km/0.25ml per minute. So they could fly 11.6km/7.21 mls in 29 minutes. By calculating the shortest flying route within a network of plants and flowers, they save energy and efficiently minimize flying time – which the fastest computers would take days to work out. Bees also have amazing memories and powerful smelling abilities to remember different aromas.

And while 174,000,000 chemical reactions have been going on in your brain – you've had to use your valuable brain power to check and delete spam

The brain generates 100,000 chemical reactions every second, and enough electrochemical energy while you're awake to power a 10-watt light bulb. It's even more active at night.

> I link, therefore I'm spammed.

The total memory capacity of your brain is estimated at 100 trillion bits of data (about 1,000 gigabytes) – about the same as the information in 500,000 large multi-volume encyclopaedias. Your brain can execute 10 quadrillion calculations per second. No computer can match it.

○ Adverts
Lost in Translation ...

➤ Our bikinis are exciting. They are simply the tops.
➤ Christmas sale. Gifts for the hard-to-find person.
➤ Tired of cleaning yourself? Let me do it.
➤ Have your ears pierced and get an extra pair to take home
➤ We can fully insult your house.
➤ Get rid of Aunts: Splat does the job in 24 hours. Stock up and save. Limit · one.

WHILE YOU'RE ... WASTING SOME OF YOUR WORK DAY

1.7 : hours

A survey by Salary.com found that a typical employee wastes an average of 1.7 hours (about 20%) of an 8 hour working day. Reasons? Work hours were too long; they didn't have enough work to do; or their work wasn't challenging enough. They used the Internet for personal reasons, and socialised with co-workers.

55% of employers have a formal policy on social media. 15.1% of Americans can't access it at work. The biggest office time-waster is gossip at the water cooler; and for 1 in 3 office workers, the favourite thing about work is the office gossip.

Man: "You know we're supposed to be discussing the sales pitch?"
Woman: "Yea, go on ... so what did she say to her boss then?"

You could be watching a comedy movie

64% of employees watch videos at work. A comedy movie is 1.5 hours; a thriller or summer blockbuster – 2 hours.

"So - just flick this switch and the accounts cover the movie so you seem to be working."

You could be searching eBay

We spend up to 1 hour 43 minutes finding fashion, home and electronic items on eBay. 50% of us don't finish online shopping.

"My goodness! I couldn't get one bid in! The boss kept me busy the whole day!"

174

WHILE YOU'RE ... FINISHING YOUR WORK DAY

The average work day is 8 hours.

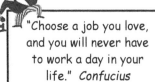

"Choose a job you love, and you will never have to work a day in your life." *Confucius*

Karen didn't quite get the idea of 'Personal Assistant'.

A typist's fingers have travelled 12.6 miles ...
... on an average workday - with the left hand doing 56% of the typing.

Typing Speed: 756 wpm, but may not be accurate.

... And so have a nurse's feet
Estimates are that nurses walk 19 km/12 miles at work in an 8 hour shift.

The world is so fast that there are days when the person who says 'it can't be done' is interrupted by the person who is doing it.

"Nurse, how exactly is my treatment going?"

Job Application Skills
Excellent memory; strong math aptitude; excellent memory; effective management skills; and very good at math.

A shrew in the Pyrenees has faced the possibility of starvation four times
A shrew can starve to death if it doesn't eat every two hours.

The International Space Station has watched five sunrises over Earth

The International Space Station travels in orbit around Earth at a speed of 28,163.52 km/h/17,500 mph – about 7.8 km/5 miles a second. So it orbits Earth – and sees the Sun rise on Earth – once every 92 minutes.

We've come from:
1609: Galileo observed Venus and Jupiter through a telescope - *to...*
1969: 20th July - man lands on the moon - *to ...*
1998: 20th November – the launch of the International Space Station

One man has made a radiator for one Rolls-Royce

It takes one man one day to make a Rolls-Royce radiator at the manufacturing plant in Goodwood, West Sussex, England.

Mistress: something between a mister and a mattress.

Did You Know?
Affairs cost American companies over $300 million/£175 million a month in lost productivity.

At Heathrow Airport, England, over 73,800 passengers have arrived and departed

The normal (pre-Covid) average number of people passing through the airport per day is 221,643.8 (9,235.2 an hour of a 24 hour day and 73,881.6 in 8 hours) of which 94% are international travellers, and 50.5% are arrivals and 49.5% - departures. Heathrow has 84 airlines serving 203 destinations in 84 countries, the most popular of which are New York (JFK) and Dubai. The daily average air transport movements are 1,303 – which is 54.29 an hour and about 1 plane for every minute of every hour of every day.

While 1 in 5 of us has been 'thinking with our eyes closed' – if it's a Wednesday

Surveys reveal that Wednesday is the most likely day for employees to nod off; and 22% of us have fallen asleep during a week at

> **Fight for the right to pretend to work.**

work. A survey of American workers also found they 'mentally' start the weekend at 2.39 pm on a Friday.

And the odds of 18 spiders to 1 human are increasing – in favour of the spiders

In most parts of the world, you're never more than 0.9 m/3 feet from a spider at any time. Research is the ratio of spiders to humans is 18:1, but many new spiders are being found all over the world – with an estimate that the 50,000 known species could double with more discoveries. There are an estimated 32,750 spiders in a house, and each spider eats 2,000 bugs a year.

"Come on now, dear. I hardly think a spider in the bath will bother me too much ... "

Spiders have 48 'knees' – 6 joints on each of their 8 legs; and are thought to have been around 300 million years ago.

'Little Miss Muffet' of nursery rhyme fame is thought to have been Ms Patience Mouffet – the daughter of Dr Thomas Mouffet, a 16th century English naturalist and physician, who believed spiders had healing powers if eaten.

WHILE YOU'RE ... DEALING WITH YOUR WORK EMAILS

13 : hours

13 hours of an average working week (33% of a 40 hour week) is spent dealing with emails. That's 650 hours of a 50 week working year. Globally, 347.3 billion emails are sent a day by 4.3 billion email users – about 4 million emails sent every second. On average, we read 25% slower from a computer screen than from paper.

A little bird sat on a telegraph wire
And said to his mates 'I declare
If wireless telegraph comes into vogue
We'll have to sit on the air'.

You're clicking your mouse nearly 700 times; moving it 35.27 m/38.57 yards/0.08 mile; and losing over 970 calories

According to Professor Fenian, Cornell University, the average person clicks their mouse 427.2 times a day. Assuming an 8 hour day – for all work including emails - that's 53.4 times an hour, and 694.2 times in 13 hours of emails. Estimates are the mouse moves 50.8 mm/2 inches between each click – totalling 35.27 m/1,388.4 inches - and 115.7 feet, 38.57 yards and 0.08 mile in 13 hours. Japanese research found we burn 1.4 calories each time we click our computer mouse. So we lose 971.88 calories in the 13 hours.

Please figure this out and get back to me asap, even though it would take me less time to do it myself than to write this email.

Over 16,000 hackers are targeting you
An estimated 30,000 websites are hacked a day worldwide – and 16,250 in 13 hours.

We apologise profusely to all our patrons who received, through unfortunate computer error, the chest measurements of members of the Female Wrestlers Association instead of the figures on sales of soyabeans to foreign countries. *(Saturday Review, UK)*

178

While the Kawahiva tribe, in the Brazilian rain forest, wander 65 km/40.3 miles in their technology-free lifestyle

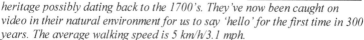

The Kawahiva (the Rio Pardo Indians) are native to the Rio Pardo of Mato Grosso, Brazil - their heritage possibly dating back to the 1700's. They've now been caught on video in their natural environment for us to say 'hello' for the first time in 300 years. The average walking speed is 5 km/h/3.1 mph.

And, in Africa, a gorilla is spending the 13 hours on its nightly sleep in its nest

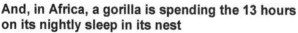

Gorillas sleep for 12 to 13 hours at night. They build their nests at sunset from leaves and branches, in trees or on the ground.

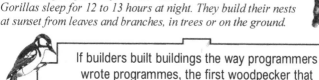

If builders built buildings the way programmers wrote programmes, the first woodpecker that came along would destroy civilization.

⏰ ⏰ ⏰ ⏰ ⏰ ⏰ ⏰ ⏰

WHILE YOU'RE ... FINISHING YOUR WORK WEEK

5 : days

The average week for a full-time worker is about 40 hours taking a cross-section of international weekly hours such as Norway and USA (38.9), UK (42.5) and Cyprus (41.7).

Job Statistics

80% - of workers think luck plays a part in how well they do their job

13% - that's how much productivity can increase with being happy at a job

41% - of workers have experienced poor mental health caused by work

Motto:
The early bird may get the worm, but the second mouse gets the cheese.

The number one peeve of workers is their colleagues 'brown-nosing'.

HURRAH FOR JAMES!

From James

James left the boss in no doubt who'd sent him a coffee treat.

They'd all just thought of a new use for the Office Manager's stapler.

The number one peeve of secretaries (43%) is employers who talk down to them.

We've all used 22,730,459,395,000 litres/5 billion gallons of petrol

The world uses 4,546,091,879,000 litres/1 billion gallons of petrol (crude oil) a day.

79,556,607.9 litres/140 million pints of best beer has been downed by the British and nearly 5 times that – by the Americans

About 15,911,321.6 litres/28 million pints of beer are drunk in the UK every day. That's over 6 Olympic-sized swimming pools worth every

Roll out the Barrel

day. (It takes about 2,500,350.5 litres/ 4.4 million pints to fill an Olympic-sized swimming pool, making 6.36 swimming pools' worth). In the USA, 63% of adults drink alcohol and 42% of them prefer beer. Americans drink 28,640,367,000 litres/6.3 billion gallons of beer a year, making 392,333,795 litres/86,301,370 gallons/690,410,960 pints in 5 days.

I always give 100% at work:
13% Monday
26% Tuesday
22% Wednesday
35% Thursday
4% Friday

You've tucked into your share of 576,000 Pot Noodles

4 are sold a second, and 576,000 in a 5 day week of 8 hour days.

Research found:

- Women working more than 35 hours a week are more likely to gain weight.
- There's 400 times more bacteria on a desktop than on a toilet seat.
- 1 in 3 married women think their husband 'forgot to mention' that he's taken a day off work to play golf.

While a toothless shark is getting ready to try out a new set of fangs

A shark can grow a new set of teeth in a week.

And someone, instead, has been hiking in the peaceful and beautiful Canadian Rockies

It takes an average of 3 to 5 days to hike the 43.5 km/27 miles of the Tonquin Valley, Canadian Rockies in Alberta.

WHILE YOU'RE ... AT YOUR JOB

| 5 : years |

The average job lasts five years.

Job Facts:

1 in 5 of us – our biggest gripe is lack of privacy at work

2 in 5 of us – would leave a higher-paid job for one with less money but makes us happier

Men who flirt at work – are usually bored or unhappy with their job

181

> "If A equals success, then the formula is: A = X + Y + Z, where X is work, Y is play, and Z is keep your mouth shut." *Albert Einstein*

Bill offered Jane a whole new solution to her filing problem.

385.5 billion kg/425,000,000 tons of paper has been used by the Americans

They use 77,110,702,900 kg/ 85,000,000 tons of paper and paperboard annually and 385,553,514,500 kg/425 million tons in 5 years.

You could have had your say on the 'job issue' in a General Election

British General Elections are every 5 years. American Presidential Elections are every 4 years.

And a TV reporter will have

walked 8,046.5 km/ 5,000 miles *You'll* walk about 1,609.3 km/1,000 miles a year if you're a TV Reporter.

Interviewer: "What party are you in the election?"
Cat: "Cat for President."
Interviewer: "And why would anyone be interested in you?"
Cat: "Well, how many talking cats have *you* met?"

A snail down your garden has lived its life

5 years is the average time it'll live. They travel at 0.047 km/h/0.01 mph.

A man opened a snail farm. It was a slow moving business.

While an Arctic Tern has flown 160,934.40 km/100,000 miles to Antarctica and back

The Arctic Tern can fly from the Arctic to the Antarctic and back – a 32,186.88 km/20,000 miles round trip - each year. It's the longest regular migration of any animal.

182

In India, a lion in the Gir Forest has made 100 kills to eat and survive

A lion will make 15 to 20 kills a year.

453,592,370,000 km/500 million tons of sand has been shifted by winds around the Earth

The wind carries about 90,718,474,000 km/100 million tons of sand around the Earth every year.

And other jobs could beckon you

Between 18 and 50 years old, a person might have 12 jobs (USA and UK). Some of the job changes could be in the same career or a new career - with an average that a person might change careers 5 to 7 times. In Australia, a person might have 17 jobs over 5 careers. Reasons for job changes could include: changed personal values, redundancy due to business closure, frustration or disillusionment with not using abilities in a job, or wanting more money.

"Money grows on the tree of persistence."
Japanese Proverb

"I'd like to be the ruler of France, please. My name's Napoleon."

"I left my last job because of a dissatisfied customer."

SITUATION WANTED:
Keen but out of work actor looking for non-appearing, non-speaking parts. *(West Highland Free Press, UK)*

You gentlemen have regained the time you used in the job – if you kissed your wife every morning

Men who kiss their wives in the morning live five years longer than those who don't. And an American insurance company found that men were less likely to have a car accident on the way to work if they were kissed before they set off.

Want to be 'job happy'?
Switch bed sides.
1 in 3 who sleeps on the left of the bed is happier about their job than 1 in 5 who sleeps on the right.

And 65% of women sleep on the left in bed.

And what was your new-born puppy when you started your job is now a 34 year old dog

A 'true dog's age' in human terms: count the first full year as 15 years, the second full year as 10 years and all the other years as 3 years. So a 5 year old dog would be 34 years old in human years.

In dog years, I'm dead.

"Money often costs too much."
Ralph Waldo Emerson

"I'm sorry Miss Smith, but alimony papers from five husbands doesn't qualify you as a divorce lawyer."

Patient: "This time, can you ask me all the questions before I have a mouth full of cotton wool?"

This Day and Age
Diary Days

This Day and Age
Diary Days

Birthdays are good for you. The more you have, the longer you live.

You're one in a million ... or rather one in 17.7 million

That's the number who share your birthday around the world. And you have a 50% chance of sharing your birthday in a group of 23 people; and a 99% chance of sharing it if you're with 75 people.

LET'S PARTY!

4 out of 5 birthday ladies are promising to give up chocolate, work harder, lose 10 lbs, stay off the wine, stop buying shoes ...

On their birthday, 81% of women plan a positive change to their life.

At a health club for women in Florence, Italy, the scales have a panel that reads 'With our apologies' – for when a person's weight goes over 57 kg/9 stone/126 lbs.

It was the sign of a great party. Nobody was actually dancing. They were just holding each other up.

> "Whatever with the past has gone,
> the best is always yet to come."
> Mark Twain

'Happy Birthday' could be sung 8,640 times

The song 'Happy Birthday' lasts an average of 10 seconds, and there's 86,400 seconds in a day. It was composed by sisters Patty and Mildred Hill in 1893. In 1988, Warner Chappel Music bought the company owning the copyright for $25 million/£14,890,700 and, from the song being used commercially, they made over $1 million/£595,628 in royalties every year. Warner claimed the US copyright would not expire until 2030. In 2016, a U S Federal Court declared that the song is no longer in copyright.

And you can be happy every hour of the day

The average person laughs between 15 and 20 times a day – average 17 times, which is about once an hour for a 16 hour waking day. Laughter expels short bursts of air up to 112.7 km/h/70 mph.

> "We should all start to live before we get too old.
> Fear is stupid. So are regrets." *Marilyn Monroe*

✦ ✦ ✦ ✦ ✦ ✦ ✦ ✦

WHILE YOU'RE ... LEAVING SCHOOL

16 : years

The minimum age a child can leave school in the UK is 16 years. In most US States, it's 16 or graduation (17 or 18 years old).

Woman: "What was your online feedback of school?"
Man: "To put video games on the curriculum."

187

You've been around the sun 16 times

A year is the time it takes the Earth to go around the Sun. The sun's gravitational pull on the Earth keeps it – and you - as part of our solar system.

> It takes courage to grow up and
> turn out to be who you really are.
> *E. E. Cummings*

You're now the person you'll show to the world

Your body's now the basic shape it will be. Your bones stop growing in length between 16 and 18 years old, with bone density – the amount of bone tissue you have – continuing to increase to 25 to 30 years old.

The world's now your oyster

In the UK, you can drive to your new job on your moped, meet friends for a pie and a pint in a bar, go home to your own apartment and watch a 16+ movie, have sex, do the lottery, and invest your money. And, at the weekend, fly a glider – and to a neighbouring country with having a passport, get married with your parents' consent, and go off on your honeymoon driving a small tractor - if that's what you fancy. And, if that wasn't enough, you can also get a pet. Different detailed laws apply to different countries.

And you've lived for half the time that Elvis was King

From Elvis's first public performance in October 1945 at the Mississippi-Alabama Fair and Dairy Show singing 'Old Shep', he performed to an audience for 32 years. His first paid performance was 30th July 1954 at the Overton Park Shell Theatre in Memphis. His last was in Indianapolis on 26th June 1977.

> "If you want immortality –
> make it." *Joaquin Miller*

The age of majority and adulthood is when you're no longer a child in law, and you're responsible for your actions and decisions independently of your parents or guardians. It's 18 years old in many countries.

"Be yourself. Everyone else is taken."
Oscar Wilde

Hello, Brain – this is me. Me ... this is Brain.

Make friends with your brain – it's now the one you'll have forever

The Key to the Door

The size and structure of the human brain stops growing at age 18; but the functioning – learning, etc – is continual. The equivalent of 3 soda cans of blood (750 to 1,000 ml/1.32 to 1.76 pints) flows through your brain each minute. With an average of 875 ml/1.54 pints a minute, that's 8,278,200 litres/1,820,949 gallons in 18 years.

The time you've lived is how long it would take to fly a jet to the sun

For a jet airliner to travel the 149,668,992 km/ 93 million miles of space to get to the Sun, it would take 18 years with the average speed of a jet as 925 kph/575 mph.

If you're American, you've put away 2,000 PB & J Sandwiches

...the number an American kid will have eaten by the age of 18.

'Cats' ran in New York for all your 18 years

At the Winter Garden Theatre on Broadway, Andrew Lloyd Webber's musical won 7 Tony Awards and had grossed $1.3 billion when it closed on 10th September 2000 after 18 years. It was based on the T S Eliot book of poems, and played 7,485 performances.

189

And new entitlements are ready for you

Although legally 'adulthood' is recognised at 21 years of age, most countries take 'majority' as being 18 years old. In the UK at 18, you can be a juror, vote, invest in businesses and your own bank accounts, and get married without your Mum and Dad's

"Gosh! You two *really* want to get to your honeymoon fast!"

consent, get tattooed, join the Army, spend the evenings at night clubs and watch porn, drink, and smoke. But - if you fall foul of the law – it's an adult jail. Different detailed laws apply to different countries.

⏱ ⏱ ⏱ ⏱ ⏱ ⏱ ⏱

WHILE YOU'RE ... NOW A MEMBER OF PLANET EARTH FOR 21 YEARS

21 : years

Your 21st birthday in the 21st century ... can you ask for more?

You've seen 420,000 TV commercials

The average number of 30-second

Man: "Do you come here often?"
Woman: "Yes – this is the third year my friend's been 21."

TV commercials seen in a year is 20,000. TV ads of the 1950s were 60 seconds long. The 30 second commercial started in the 1970s. Ads are now 15 seconds to 5 minutes long.

Other creatures have shared your 21 years, around the world

Animals that can live in the wild for about 21 years include the Gila monster, wildebeest, bald eagle and the grizzly bear.

190

At 21, the past, the present and the world is connecting with you

The old Latin alphabet had 21 characters. There are 21 animals and birds unique to New Zealand. 21 is the atomic number of the chemical element scandium. 21 is considered to be one of the lucky numbers. In numerology, 21 represents: creative self-expression, optimism, inspiration, relationships and diplomacy. 21 is the highest-winning point total in Blackjack. The 21st Amendment repealed Prohibition in the USA. The total number of spots on a 6-sided die

"Keep 'em coming. I'm starting the party with a bang … a 21 gin salute."

is 21 (1+2+3+4+5+6). There are 21 sun rays on the Kurdistan flag. And ... a 21-gun salute honours royalty or leaders of countries.

It's been summer on Uranus right through your life …

… or Autumn, Winter, or Spring. On Uranus, each pole has around 42 years of continuous sunlight, followed by 42 years of darkness. So each season on Uranus lasts 21 Earthly years.

And the Stones have been rolling nearly three times as long as you've been alive

The first single of the Rolling Stones was 'Come On/I Want to be Loved' released on 7th July 1963. The most recent – released on 22nd July 2020 – is 'Scarlet'. They've been releasing singles for 57 years.

I am not here to change the world. I am changing the world because I am here.

WHILE YOU'RE ... CELEBRATING YOUR QUARTER OF A CENTURY

3.36 billion people in the world are your age or under
42% of the world's population is under 25.

In the UK, there's now the same number of Sylvanian toy caravans as real ones
Over 500,000 Sylvanian Family caravans were bought in 25 years – the same number as actual touring caravans in the UK.

*"Jump out of a cardboard cake, they said.
But I'm on a diet, I said."*

Men begin to look for a bald patch
The average age of balding men going to hair clinics is just under 25 years. Going bald is the number one fear of men, and 42% of them feel depressed when they start to lose their hair.

Stuart hoped the International Bald Society would find a bare spot so he could join them for their trip to Hawaii.

"I do not consider myself bald; I am just taller than my hair."
Lucius Annaeus Seneca

In Beijing, someone who's been sleeping their way through the Imperial Palace, is just coming out of it
The Imperial Palace is the largest in the world and, if you slept in a different room every night, it would take you 25 years.

Some of the US cash is due for retirement
The lifespan of an American coin is 25 to 30 years.

In Northern Australia, an eel has been swimming around reeds and water lilies, by black cormorants, dragon lizards, dwarf tree frogs and bats, waiting to breed

The Long-finned Eel (Anguilla Reinhardtii) lives for up to 25 years in the freshwater Lake Barrine of the Maar Volcanoes of Northern Queensland before dropping over waterfalls and 762 m/2,500 ft down to the ocean to breed, lay eggs and die.

The star Epsilon Aurigae is due for its eclipse, 2,000 light years away

Epsilon Aurigae, otherwise known as Haldus, has a huge dark disk orbiting it and, about every 27 years, this disk eclipses it for about 2 years (640 to 730 days) with a low amplitude pulse for about 66 days. If the disk started its orbit when you were born, the eclipse is due.

And UFO's aren't so popular

In 1954, the mayor of Châteauneuf-du-Pape in France passed a law banning all flying saucers from landing or taking off in the area.

An American study found the number of UFO sightings has decreased by just over 90% over the last 25 years.

☺ ☺ ☺ ☺ ☺ ☺ ☺ ☺

WHILE YOU'RE ... PARTYING AS A 30-YEAR-OLD

30 : years

You've spun round on the Earth 10,957.50 times

The Earth rotates 365.25 times a year – the number of days. The actual rotation time is about 23 hours and 56 minutes with the solar day being almost exactly 24 hours, because of the distance the Earth moves in its orbit round the Sun. So 365.25 times a year x 30 years is 10,957.50 rotations.

Woman: "I've already given you my undying love. Very soon, I might have to frisk you for my birthday present."

And now …

You've reached your cognitive peak; have the best ability to recognise faces; have a 70% chance of peaking at happiness (6% in college years and 16% in childhood); make friends that last longer; peak at sport performance and endurance; earn more and have more career satisfaction; have more satisfying sex; have ground-breaking new ideas; start shrinking; start losing 7,000 brain cells a day - never replaced; and outlive the Egyptians who mostly died by 30 years old, 3,000 years ago.

"His wife's just texted him. The doctor said it's not indigestion and the baby's due in six months."

And it's about the average age for a woman to have her first child

In 2022, the average age at which women had their first child was 31 years old. For men, it was 33.6 years.

☺ ☺ ☺ ☺ ☺ ☺ ☺ ☺

WHILE YOU'RE … FAB AT 40 YEARS OLD

40 : years

"Every man over forty is a scoundrel."
George Bernard Shaw

"Let's call your Birthday cocktail 'Stop Counting'."
"Great idea! Keep 'em coming!"

Big Bertha's been on Earth longer than you

'Big Bertha' is the largest piece of moon rock stored at the Lunar Sample Laboratory Facility (LSLF) at NASA's Lyndon B. Johnson Space Center in Houston, Texas. It's Lunar Sample 14321. It was returned during the Apollo 14 mission (31st January to 9th February 1971), and is the third largest sample returned by any Apollo mission. It's grey with patches of black and white, and it's between 4 and 4.5 billion years old. So through all your years of nursery, school, college, jobs and parties – a piece of moon rock has been kept safely in Texas, USA ... probably without you knowing it.

And, in less than your 40 years, we'll be living on the Moon

The European Space Agency (ESA) has mapped out designs for a Moon base, and tested a 3D worlded structure that can use lunar materials with additional Earth structures. It's estimated that humans will live there within 40 years.

"If you make the 'there's no atmosphere' joke once more, I'm moving back to Earth."

> **The only way we can live our life to the fullest is if we understand that we don't have all the time in the world.**

You've become FAB

F*lush – men earn the most in their mid-40s; women – at 39.* **A***stute – and empathetic, with the most understanding of someone's emotions.* **B***est – doing your best work now.*

If you're a Brit – you're the average age. If you're American – you're almost the average age to be bankrupt by medical expenses

The average Briton is 40.7 years old; Americans file for medical bankruptcy at an average age of 44.9 years old.

But you can still win a Nobel Prize – nine 40 year olds have

They were in Physics, Chemistry, and Peace; and Nobel Prize-winning research is done at an average age of 40 years.

> At the age of 10, Albert Einstein was told by a schoolmaster that he would 'never amount to very much'.

WHILE YOU'RE ...
CELEBRATING LIVING
THROUGH THE LAST **50** YEARS

It's your Golden Jubilee Birthday, half-century and anniversary of five decades – and you can call yourself a quinquagenarian.

Priscilla thought a BYOB party meant Bring Your Own Body.

If you haven't grown up by age 50, you don't have to.

What was a baby oak tree has now started to produce acorns
Oak trees don't produce acorns until they are at least 50 years old.

When you were born in the 1970s:
Inflation rates were 7.25% in the USA and 6.4% in the UK.
The average cost of a house was $23,600 and £4,975.

While the world was changing
Britain went decimal while Watergate brewed in the USA. Women wore hot pants and fought for their rights. Barbie matched Action Man, and there were Space Hoppers, the space shuttle and 'Space Invaders'. There was Abba and punk rock, Pink Floyd and Queen. The world opened up with Concorde and the Boing 747, and Microsoft and Apple. The Beatles disbanded and the Florida Disney Resort opened. We were groovy with platform boots and flares, a digital watch and a Sony Walkman, and drove a car like Starsky and Hutch. On our colour TV, we watched the Muppet Show, the Flintstones, Bewitched and Hawaii Five-O. We used VHS Video Recorders not to miss Dallas, and got a microwave meal before we went out to watch Star Wars or Jaws on the 'big screen' and then headed to our waterbed.

And there are now more women behind the lens than men

50 years ago, men took the most photos – now women do. But a survey revealed that women like guys with a hobby of photography.

You're half as likely to catch a cold than a teenager is

Teenagers catch colds twice as often as people over the age of 50.

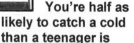

Your toilet should be giving up the ghost about now

The life expectancy of a modern toilet is 50 years.

Mastering the digital camera was easy. Sorting out the USB cable – now that was hard ...

And you could invite a chimp to your birthday celebrations

Chimpanzees can live about 50 years in the wild.

🕐 🕐 🕐 🕐 🕐 🕐 🕐 🕐

WHILE YOU'RE ... CHEERING AT BECOMING 60 YEARS OLD

60 : years

"To get back my youth I would do anything in the world, except take exercise, get up early, or be respectable."
Oscar Wilde

They all had instructions to stop filling her glass when Aunt Maude started with her maracas.

197

Some of what you've lived through is ...

The Vietnam War, the assassination of President John F Kennedy, Cassius Clay beating Sonny Liston, Flower Power and Woodstock, the Eurotunnel between the UK and France, Fights between Mods and Rockers in Brighton, UK, Nelson Mandela spending 18 years in prison, and Dr. Martin Luther King, Jr receiving the Nobel Peace Prize. There were the Rolling Stones, the Beatles, Bob Dylan, Elvis Presley, Cliff Richard, Bob Marley, Simon & Garfunkel and Jimi Hendrix, Radio Caroline, Roald Dahl, Elizabeth Taylor and Richard Burton, and Ella Fitzgerald. And you've seen Mary Poppins and Harry Potter, and John Wayne, Doris Day and Steve McQueen. There's been 8-track tapes, tape recorders, video recorders, DVD's and Blue Ray; and The Prisoner, Monty Python's Flying Circus, Lassie, Bonanza, The Man from Uncle, and I Dream of Jeannie. There's been the Telstar Satellite, cash dispensers, heart pacemakers, the World Wide Web, moon landings and lasers – and, of course, the mini skirt and the Austin Mini Cooper.

Bring back the Sixties

On 21st July 1969, when Neil Armstrong landed on the moon, the Central Electricity Generating Board in Britain had a surge demand for power equivalent to a city of a million people. Over half the UK population and over 720 million around the world watched the historic event.

While in Pennsylvania, the Groundhog has been wrong about spring 3 out of 5 times

Over 60 years, the famous American woodchuck has been accurate in predicting the coming of spring an estimated 35% to 40%. Since 1887, it's been right just 39% of the time. The largest Groundhog Day celebration is held in Punxsutawney, Pennsylvania, USA. On 2nd February – if it's cloudy when the groundhog comes out of its burrow, spring will come early. A sunny day means it'll see its shadow, and it'll stay wintry for another six weeks.

And there's a cactus in Arizona that has to be older than you before it can grow

The saguaro cactus in the Sonoran Desert only grows branches when it's 60 to 75 years old. It can grow to 15.24 m/50 feet and 200 years old.

198

You're one of 959,490,000 with a grey hair

A survey found that only 10% of people aged 60 and over don't have a grey hair. There are 1,066.1 million people aged 60 to 100 years, worldwide.

60 year old men have a 3 in 5 chance they'll snore; women - a 2 in 5 chance

A regular snoring level is 60 decibels – about as loud as normal speech; heavy snoring can be over 80 decibels – about the level of a pneumatic drill going through concrete.

Musically speaking – snoring is sheet music

You can't snore and dream at the same time.

But you've become more than 'older and wiser'

You have the most wisdom of all age groups (at 60 to 90 years), but also better life satisfaction than at 55 years old, and an excellent use of language – the highest scores in multiple-choice vocabulary tests (at 60 and 70 years).

Matchbox has turned out 3 billion of your favourite toy cars

If placed bumper-to-bumper they'd circle the Earth six times.

Determination won out. They got over-60's dangerous sports insurance for their new hobby of Rally Racing.

And the world has 15,000 more crop circles

About 250 crop patterns appear around the world each year. They were mentioned in 1678, and again from 1966, peaking in the 1980s and 1990s. Explanations for them include: aliens, time travellers, wind patterns, Earth ley

line energy fields and, in the 1980s - the enthusiastic sexual activity of randy hedgehogs supposedly caused them. A lot of crop circles are hoaxes, but some can't be explained.

199

You've become a Centenarian Super Star

And you got there by being: resilient, adaptable to change, positive, productive, physically active, self-confident, happy, close to family and friends, and decisive - if not stubborn!

Congratulations

And the King is sending you a celebratory card

Woman: "You'd better get some gin for Grandma. She's going to need it! The caterers sent this and she's expecting to celebrate her 100th!"

Centenarians, in the Commonwealth and UK Territories, can apply online for a card. 573,000 people worldwide celebrate their 100th 'party of parties'.

Since you were born, Venice has sunk over 23 cm/9 inches

Woman: "The local paper's written about Gramps' 100th – and that he was called 'Gigolo Jo' in the Fifties. He used to say 'Like father, like son'. Is there something you want to tell me?"

It's sunk 24 cm/9.44 inches in the last century – almost 3.5 times faster than the previous 7 cm/2.75 inches per 100 years. Venice has 177 canals, and 417 bridges, 72 – private.

The Himalayas are 127 cm/50 inches higher

The world's tallest mountains are now even taller. They grow by about 1.3 cm/0.5 inch a year, because of the pressure exerted by two of Earth's continental plates (the Eurasian plate and the Indo-Australian plate) pushing against each other.

The sea is 18.5 cm/7.3 inches higher

The sea level has risen 16 to 21 cm/ 6.3 to 8.3 ins – an average of 18.5 cm/7.3 inches - over the past century and this level is expected to increase.

Neptune has made just over two thirds of its revolution round the sun

Neptune's revolution period is 164.8 Earth years. It's the most distant planet from the sun.

The US tax code is over six times fatter

Its size has increased by 650% in the last 100 years, and it's now ten times the size of the Bible.

"Don't try to get round me. The answer's still 'no'. I will not be your floozy as a taxable expense."

The world invented tax before money - in 3200 BC in Sumeria, Mesopotamia, and 2,600 years before the first coins of 600 BC in Greece.

I was spending so much time with my accountant, that it was cheaper to marry him, divorce and pay alimony.

And there are fireworks out in space to celebrate your 100th

Somewhere in the Universe, in typical galaxies like the Milky Way, a massive star should end its life as a supernova about every 100 years.

201

Being in the Moment
Miscellaneous

"I could get knocked down
by a bus tomorrow."

Being in the Moment
Miscellaneous

WHILE YOU'RE ... IN ANY MOMENT – IN A JIFFY

0.01 : seconds

A 'jiffy' has different meanings in computer science, physics, chemistry and electrical engineering, but is now widely accepted as being 1/100th of a second.

In 1 jiffy ... A cough travels 0.44 metres/18 inches – and a hawk moth,

in a Peruvian rain forest, can travel a third of the distance - 0.15 metres/6 inches

An explosive cough can travel at 160

One sure thing that's gone in a jiffy.

km/h/100 mph - 44.44 metres/146.7 feet a second, and 0.44 metres/1.47 feet in a jiffy - 0.01 of a second. A hawk moth can fly at 54.7 km/h /34 mph, which is 929.9 metres/2,992 feet a minute, 15.8 metres/49.87 feet a second and 0.15 metres/0.49 feet in a jiffy of 0.01 second.

In 2 jiffies ... It's the near-

instant moment you feel the pain when you stub your toe – as fast as a water shrew attacks a prey

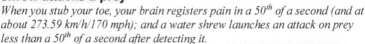

When you stub your toe, your brain registers pain in a 50th of a second (and at about 273.59 km/h/170 mph); and a water shrew launches an attack on prey less than a 50th of a second after detecting it.

'Carpe Diem' – Seize the Day.
Their high metabolic rate means water shrews need to eat their weight in food a day. So, when they see prey, they can't afford to hesitate.

"Know the true value of time; snatch, seize and enjoy every moment of it." *Lord Chesterfield*

And it takes 2.5 jiffies for a rocket to ignite

The minimum ignition time for a rocket motor is 24 milliseconds - 0.024 seconds - about 2.5 jiffies.

The time interval between gear changes in the Ferrari FXX is 10 jiffies

The time is 100 milliseconds (0.1 seconds).

In an Australian forest, a death adder strikes and recoils in 15 jiffies

It can attack its prey with venom and recoil back to its strike position in under 0.15 of a second.

In Canada, a star-nosed mole snatches a bite in under 30 jiffies

It can detect, catch and eat food faster than the human eye can follow – in under 0.3 seconds.

ö ö ö ö ö ö ö

WHILE YOU'RE ... WATCHING THE KING'S CHRISTMAS MESSAGE

| 9 : minutes |

The King's Christmas Message to the Empire lasts about 9 minutes.

Naughty or Nice?
Gentlemen - 1 in 4 of you lie about where you bought a gift during the Christmas holidays.
Ladies – you buy 38% more padded bras during the holiday season.
And ... 1 in 20 of us all has faked an illness to get off work to go Christmas shopping.

On the list of 'life stresses', Christmas shopping in December comes 4th.

Stress: the confusion created when your mind overrides your body's basic desire to choke the living daylights out of someone who desperately needs it.

The coffee's brewed
It takes 7 to 10 minutes till the coffee's ready in an electric percolator.

Brits will eat 144,000 Smarties chocolates
16,000 individual Smarties are eaten every minute in the UK. It takes 22 hours to make Smarties from scratch.

You can play with the kids
Parents spend an average of nine minutes playing with their children on Christmas day.

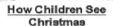

How Children See Christmas
Christmas beats all other events, including birthdays, as being important to kids, and 40% plan what they want 2 to 3 months before it. 51% of 4 to 9 year olds think Santa is the Christmas present giver.

Darling, let the kids play too. It's their turn with the train set now.

And someone's just finished inflating the air mattress for their Christmas visitors
With an electric pump, it takes 8.9 minutes to fill a twin-sized air mattress (99 x 187.96 x 20.32 cm/39 x 74 x 8 ins) with a pump using 0.51 cu m/18 cu ft per minute.

Three phrases that sum up Christmas are: 'Peace on Earth', 'Goodwill to All Men' and 'Batteries not Included'.

WHILE YOU'RE ... AT YOUR CHURCH SERVICE

Church services range in length from 45 minutes to 2 hours, and average one hour.

TV or Church – you'll burn the same calories in an hour (68 for a 68.04 kg/150 lb person).

"Yo, Sis. Still the Skating Nun?"

"Yep. Can't quit the habit."

❄ **In the bleak midwinter – a snowflake started its journey from the heavens when you went into church, and landed at your feet when you came out**

A snowflake can take up to an hour to land. All snowflakes have six sides, and the odds of two snowflakes being exactly the same are 1 in 1 million trillion with an estimated 1 trillion, trillion, trillion different types of snowflakes.

There will be a procession next Sunday afternoon in the grounds of the Monastery; but if it rains in the afternoon, the procession will take place in the morning.
(Irish Parish Bulletin)

❄ *Snowmen fall from heaven ... unassembled*

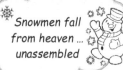

About every couple of pews, someone's checking their cell phone during the service
Almost 1 in 10 of churchgoers does.

The St. Cecelia Singers were honoured last week by the BBC when a television presenter invited them to take part in the programme 'Let's have a good sin.'
(Chester Chronicle, UK)

1 in 3 of us is having an hour of de-stressing

For 1 in 3 of us, religion is the second biggest stress-relief - behind personal

A preacher was getting into her sermon on drink. "If I had all the beer in the world, I'd take it and throw it into the river", she said. Then, with even more enthusiasm, she voiced loudly "And if I had all the wine in the world, I'd take it and throw it into the river". And, ending on a crescendo, she yelled "And if I had all the whiskey in the world, I'd take it and throw it into the river". She sat down. The choir leader then stood up, hesitatingly announcing with a smile, "For our closing song, let us sing Hymn No. 365: 'Shall We Gather at the River'."

relationships. Research shows that a church service can lower blood pressure for both men and women, with a greater fall in blood pressure for more frequent church-goers.

And the world has lost 17 species of plants or animals to extinction

The Dodo Bird

According to one study, plant and animal species are becoming extinct at the rate of 17 an hour. 99% of all animal species that ever lived on Earth are now extinct.

But …

New species are being discovered, including a lizard (bent-toed gecko) in Vietnam, giant tarantula (Poecilotheria rajaei) in Sri Lanka, a shrew (Thor's hero shrew) in Africa and a new carnivorous mammal species (the Olinguito) – the first such species discovered in over 40 years. Scientists have also rejuvenated cells of Rheobatrachus silus, a species of frog extinct since 1983; and 'brought back to life' 400 year old bryophyte specimens (green moss-like plants) that were left behind by retreating glaciers in Canada.

Don't be afraid to try something new. Amateurs built the Ark; professionals built the Titanic.

10% of us believe Friday the 13th is an unlucky day. The fear dates back to the late 1800's. You usually don't have to go through your Friggatriskaidekaphobia more than a couple of times a year, and no year has more than three 'Friday the 13th's'.

It costs $900 million/ £535 million

The fear of bad luck on Friday the 13th, and people not functioning normally at work, costs businesses $900 million/£535 million on that one day.

Where it all started?

"What day is it?"

"Friday the 13th. Why?"

You've got an extra 0.00000002 seconds to go through that could change your whole day

Each day is longer than the one it follows by 0.00000002 seconds because the Earth's spin is gradually slowing down.

You can distract yourself for a few Friday the 13th's

13th October 2023 – I didn't make it up – it really is International Day For Failure, so join in Silly Sayings Day (USA) to amuse yourself instead. 13th September 2024 – in America it's Kids Take Over the Kitchen Day but it's also Positive Thinking Day, which might help. 13th December 2024 – it's Pick a Pathologist Pal Day in the USA – serenade them on your Stradivarius cos it's also World Violin Day. 13th June 2025 – is a brilliant day for Friday the 13th, being the Kitchen Klutz of America Day – so klutz all you like. 13th February 2026 - it's International Condom Day, and in America, you can change your name before or after celebrating it, with Get a Different Name Day. 13th March 2026 - laugh in the face of bad luck with National Open an Umbrella Indoors Day (USA). 13th November 2026 – it's World Kindness Day, and we'll all need a hug because, according to Physicist Heinz von Foerster, it's also Doomsday.

But the date doesn't change the wait … and together, we're all wasting the equivalent of 84,760 years daily - waiting for downloads

The average computer user spends 9 minutes every day waiting for files and web screens to download. There are 4.95 billion Internet users worldwide. So it's the equivalent of 84,760 years 3 months 1 week 3 days 1 hour 55 minutes and 12 seconds that we're collectively waiting for downloads - every day.

Never let a computer know you're in a hurry.

Building a Web

62.5% of the world's population is an Internet user, with the highest numbers in China, India and the USA. The recommended maximum time delay for a person waiting for a web page to load is 250 milliseconds (0.25 secs).

We've come from:
300 BC: the Babylonians invented zero - *to …*
100 BC: binary numbers were first written - *to …*
1937: the use of binary code in computers - *to …*
2010: 3rd April – the iPad was launched

And it's normal on this – or any day –that:

Ladies – you have a 20% chance of accidentally dropping your make-up in the toilet.

1 in 10,000 of us could be injured by a toilet seat.

(And 30,000 Americans are injured by toilets every year.)

You could be the 1 in 25 who forgets where you parked.

3 out of 5 Brits will fail their driving test.

You'll forget 80% of what you learn in the day.

You have the same international odds of a 'straight up' bet at the roulette wheel.

(That's 36 to 1 (French) and 37 to 1 (American).)

Luck is when preparation meets opportunity.

209

WHILE YOU'RE ... WAITING FOR A SPELL TO WORK

88.5 : days

For a spell to take the desired effect, it varies from a few days to 12 weeks – mostly accepted as 3 moon phases – approximately 88.5 days.

What if your wish didn't come true because someone made a wish that nobody else gets their wish?

You didn't cross the Gardening Club Committee. They knew a thing or two about mushrooms ...

You could jog half way round the world

Assuming a pace of 9.66 km/h/6 mph, it would take 4,150.26 hours to jog the whole circumference of 40,075.16 km/24,901.55 miles at the equator, or 172.93 days, of which 86.5 would get you to the half way refreshment pit stop.

A minister exorcised a house in Sherborne, Dorset, after two women summoned Elvis Presley's spirit with a Ouija board. The women, suffering from shock, reported the appearance as Presley's first visit to Britain. *(Southend Evening Echo, UK)*

While it's half a day on Mercury

A full Mercurian day (like our 24 hours) lasts 176 Earth days – about 6 Earth months.

And about half way through the

'dark days' at the South Pole

The South Pole has no sun for 182 days each year.

Being happy is the best and sweetest revenge.

210

In 1978, a lady pronounced herself a witch, and went to work with her spells to be a complete failure. She cursed Nottingham Forest, an English Football Club – and they won the League Championship and Football League Cup, with the longest unbeaten run in the history of English football. They then went on to win the European Cup for two years in succession.

And you've made over 3.2 million decisions

We make 37,058.4 decisions in an 18 hour day - nearly 1 a second - and 3,279,668.4 in 88.5 days. We make 226.7 decisions a day on food alone, and also decide on work, spending money, friendships and relationships, TV channels, what to wear, etc. But our mental energy has a limit and decreases during the day, and 'Decision Fatigue' can kick in. Then decisions are harder to make and our brain might take a shortcut – by which we act recklessly and impulsively, or do nothing and avoid choice.

🕰 🕰 🕰 🕰 🕰 🕰 🕰

WHILE YOU'RE ... LIVING THROUGH YOUR DEATH YEAR

1 : year

Every 365 days you live through the day you will die. You might know your birthday, but you don't know what day you will die. So you live through each one of the possibilities during a year.

Top Tips

Head for Japan. *It has the least number of murders, and avoid El Salvador – the highest number of murders.*

If you're in America – vacation in August in Europe, Asia or anywhere else. *In the US, murder is committed most frequently in August.*

And avoid trees in America. *You have a 1 in 6,755,102 chance of being hit by lightning.*

"Shun death is my advice."
Robert Browning

211

"We have two lives, and the second begins when we realize we only have one."
Confucius

You'll spend 5.5 hours getting cash, with 2 out of 5 of you talking to the 'hole in the wall'

The average person spends this time each year getting cash from a bank, ATM, cash advance facility etc. And 40% of us talk to the ATM.

Nearly 39 million planes will take off and land around the world

There are 38.9 million airline flights in the world annually. There are 8,000 to 20,000 planes flying worldwide at any moment; and, in the USA, you're 18.4 times more likely to be injured in the car on the way to the airport than you are flying in the plane. The odds in a year in the USA are: dying in a car – 1 in 47,852; dying in a plane – 1 in 879,482. But what if you could fill your car with the entire fuel of a plane?

If you used a car instead of a plane ...

... you could drive 86.5 times around the surface of the world on the amount of fuel in a Boeing 747-8 jet. Using a car doing 11.9 kmpl/28 mpg, and that a plane carries 291,199.92 litres/64,055 gallons of fuel, and the circumference at the equator is 40,074 m/ 24,901 miles – it's 86.47 times around the world in a car. Sadly car and plane fuel are not interchangeable – yet ...

You ladies will have five duvet days in the year

A woman clocks up an average five days a year in her PJ's – just you, the duvet and ... they know your number if they want you.

If you're a Brit, you have a 0.002 chance of moving out of the city

There are 53,369,083 adults in the UK (18 years plus). Over 100,000 of them quit the city every year for country life.

Now let's see if they can deliver a pizza here in 10 minutes or your money back.

Nearest Town
500 km

Squirrels will make sure they'll always be trees

Worldwide, every year, several million trees grow because squirrels forget where they buried their nuts which then plant themselves.

And it's the world, but not as we know it:

The moon's going to be 3.8 cm/1.5 inches further away from the Earth by the end of the year

The moon's orbit is moving 3.8 cm/1.5 inches – about the length of a matchstick - further away from the Earth, and the Earth is pushing it away more quickly than in the past 50 million years.

And Mexico City's going to sink 46 cm/18 inches

Mexico City's sinking because water's been pumped from the aquifer underneath it for the 18 million residents to use when its natural springs were exhausted. The sinking in the centre has been slowed to 2.5 cm/1 inch annually; that of the suburbs is 45.7 to 61 cm/18 to 24 inches a year. To date, it's sunk 9.14 m/30 feet.

And New York will weigh less than a year ago

The granite that's removed to make way for the foundations of a new building in New York weighs more than the actual building. So Manhattan's getting lighter each year.

"If you knew that you were going to die tonight, or merely that you would have to go away and never return, would you, looking upon men and things for the last time, see them in the same light that you have hitherto seen them? Would you not love as you never yet have loved?" *Maurice Maeterlinck*

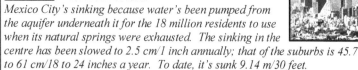

In the US, you'll see more than a million television cereal ads

Annual cereal television ads in the USA - 1.3 million.

If you're a guy – nearly half of you will try a new beer sometime in the year

Just over 40% of men try a new beer at least once a year.

"Well, if you want a holiday but you don't like to travel - maybe sit in the garden with a few foreign beers?"

If you're a woman, you've got a 1 in 10 chance of being wolf-whistled

10% of women have been whistled at by a man in the past 12 months.

213

If you live like a rock star, you're gambling on seeing 43

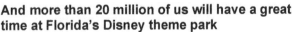

European rock stars live an average 35 years; American ones – an average 42 years, and they double their chances of dying younger than the average 'three scores years and ten' (research: Liverpool John Moores University).

> "Of all sad words of tongue or pen, the saddest are these: 'It might have been'."
> *John Greenleaf Whittier*

And more than 20 million of us will have a great time at Florida's Disney theme park

Over 20 million visitors go to the Disney Magic Kingdom Park, Orlando Florida, yearly.

So when's the last time you had fun?
1 in 5 of us can't remember.

"We are always getting ready to live but never living."
Ralph Waldo Emerson

WHILE YOU'RE ... NOW PRESUMED DEAD

7 : years

In most countries, someone must be missing for 7 years to be legally dead.

The most 'popular' time for dying? From 2 am to 5 am – also the most common time for babies to be born.
The best song for a funeral? Wham!'s 'Wake Me Up Before You Go-Go' - as voted for in a survey of school children.

214

Man: "I saved you from a sinking ship, so what now?"
Woman: "You forgot my birthday."

You've grown a new skeleton; and all but 2% of your atoms have been replaced seven times

The human body grows the equivalent of a new skeleton every seven to nine years; and every year about 98% of the atoms in your body are replaced.

And if you return home – half your friends will be new ones

You lose and replace about half your close friends every seven years or so.

Make new friends,
but keep the old.
One is silver and
the other is gold.

"So, did your ex-boss agree to be your Facebook friend?"

Or ... if you really do die - a child, born when you first went missing, has now developed his or her best ability to see your ghost

Paranormal experts say we reach the peak of our ability to see ghosts at the age of seven.

A poll revealed that 1.8 million dead people are on the American electoral roll.

And the Corpse Flower may be blooming

The Titan Arum (Amorphophallus titanum) blooms every 6 to 10 years. It's native to Indonesia's Sumatra, reaching up to 3.66 m/12 ft with a flower over 1.52 m/5 ft tall and 1.22 m/4 ft across, with a phallic-like spadix in the centre, but with a very uninviting smell that attracts carrion-eating beetles to pollinate it.

"Run from what's comfortable. Forget safety. Live where you fear to live. Destroy your reputation. Be notorious. I have tried prudent planning long enough. From now on I'll be mad." *Rumi*

"Whatever you can do or dream you can – begin it. Boldness has genius, power and magic in it. Begin it now."

Johann Wolfgang von Goethe

The Journey of a Lifetime

70 Years

The Journey of a Lifetime
70 Years

In the classic 'three score years and ten' of a lifetime, we have 2,207,520,000 seconds to love, laugh, discover, dream, and achieve all we want from the time of our lives. Much of our time is spent on the functions of living. What's left, after sleeping,

 eating, working, and all necessities that are taken out of those 70 years, is the time we have to accomplish everything, have fun, and be with family and friends.

I've analysed how those precious seconds are used; some in commitments and some frittered away without us noticing.

Unless otherwise stated, the following figures apply to 52 years of adult lifetime from ages 18 to 70 years. They're taken from research and surveys and are for the average person. In the calculations, I assume that all remains the same in our lifestyles – which, of course, it won't, with life changes; but the totals are a guideline as to where the time of our life goes.

The figures are calculated, in total, based on a year of 365 days and a month of 30 days. For example, the time we spend working is 11.43 years. This isn't that we only work for 11.43 out of a possible working life of up to 52 years but that, with all the work time added together, it's the equivalent of spending 11.43 full years of 24 hour days of our lifetime at work.

The time dreaming is obviously part of the time we are sleeping. But some of what we do in our lives overlaps. Time on the Internet could be work or leisure time pursuits, and work may be in the same hours as dieting.

I hope this is enlightening, interesting and fun.

> "May you live all the days of your life."
> *Jonathan Swift*

Your Body

Toilet:
Toilet visits: 130,000 (2,500 times a year)
Amount of toilet paper used: 3,073.47 rolls (57 sheets a day, 352 sheets a roll)
Urine produced: 54,553 litres/12,000 gallons
Time of post-toilet hand-washing: 3 weeks 1 day 13 hours 41 minutes (15 seconds minimum each of above 130,000 times)
Breaking wind (70 years): Amount: 25,550 litres/44,961 pints (1 litre/1.76 pints in 24 hours); No. of times: 357,700 (average 14 times a day)
Waiting to use the bathroom/toilet: 3 months 1 week 2 days (7.5 minutes a day)
Time spent on the toilet: 3 years

Hair:
Total beard length grown – Men: 6.6 m/7 yards 8 inches (12.7 cm/5 inches a year)
Length of face hair shaved – Men: 8.5 m/28 feet
Length of nose hair grown: 1.8 m/6 feet
Hair: No. lost: 1,328,600 hairs (about 70 a day of 100,000); Length grown: 491,667.8 m/19,357,000 inches/305.5 miles (including accounting for number of hairs lost)

Brain:
Amount of information retained by the brain: 1 quadrillion bits
Number of thoughts: 1,328,600,000 (70,000 a day)
Number of decisions: 703,368,432 (37,058.4 in 18 hour day)
Brain (70 years): No. of brain cells lost: 89,425,000 (7,000 a day from 35 years); No. of chemical reactions: 220,752,000,000,000 (about 220.7 trillion) (100,000 a second); Amount of blood through the brain: 32,193,000,000 ml/32,193,000 litres/56,651,760.08 pints/7,081,470 gallons (750 to 1000 ml/1.32 to 1.76 pints per minute – average 875 m/1.54 pints a minute)

Sleeping:
Asleep (70 years): 23 years 4 months (8 hours a night)
Dreaming: No. of dreams: 102,200 (1,460 a year); Amount of time: 4 years 4 months 2 weeks 3 days (1.5 hours a night)
Nocturnal erections – Men: 75,920 (4 a night); Time spent: 4 years 4

months 6 days (2 hours a night)
Falling asleep: 3 months (7 minutes a night)
Insomnia: 7 years
Loss of sleep through worry: 2 years 2 months (15 days a year)
Other:
Percentage of developed ovarian eggs – Women: 0.07% (350 (average from 300 to 400) developed of 500,000)
Saliva produced: 28,413 litres/50,000 pints/6,250 gallons
Water drunk: 45,460 to 54,552 litres/10,000 to 12,000 gallons
Number of words spoken: 303,680,000 (16,000 words a day, both sexes)
Smiling/Laughing: No. of times: 434,350 (average 17 times a day, 70 years); Amount of time: 3 months 2 weeks 1 day (6 minutes a day, 70 years); Men thinking about smiling: 189,800 times (10 times a day, 52 years)
Loss of height: 5 cm/2 inches
Skin: No. of new skins: 1,213.3 (cells shed and re-grow every 21 days, 70 years); Amount of dead skin: 188.69 kg/416 lbs (3.6 kg/8 lbs a year)
Heart & circulation (70 years): No. of heart beats: 3 billion (101,000 a day); Quantity of blood: 378,541,178.4 litres/800 million pints; Blood circuits around the body: 25,550,000 times (1,000 times a day); Blood cells destroyed and made: 4,415,040,000,000,000 (4.4 quadrillion) (2 million a second)
Total length of eyelashes shed: 30.48 m/100 feet
Growth of fingernails (70 years): One nail: 2.13 m/84 inches/2.3 yards; Ten nails: 21.34 m/840 inches/23.33 yards (2.54 mm/0.1 inch a month)
Eyes (70 years): No. of times muscles focus: 2,555,000,000 (100,000 times a day); No. of times blinking: 441,504,000 (16 times a minute, 18 hour days); Time spent blinking: 2 years 9 months 2 weeks 4 days (0.2 seconds each); Time adjusting eyes to the dark: 1 year 5 months 8 days 12 hours (40 minutes a night); Putting in contact lenses: 2 days 5 hours (10 seconds a day, 52 years)
Air breathed (70 years): Amount: 255,500,000 litres/56,202,119.7 gallons (10,000 litres/2,199.7 gallons a day); No. of breaths: 511,000,000 (average 20,000 a day)
Number of steps: 81,775,330 (4,308.5 steps a day)
Number of finger joint flexes: 24 million

Health & Wellbeing

Teeth:
Brushing teeth (70 years): 2 months 12 days (2 minutes twice daily)
Water for rinsing teeth: 310,270.8 litres/68,250 gallons
Mouthwash: 6 days 14 hours (30 seconds once a day)
Teeth lost with smoking: 10.4 teeth (a pack-a-day smoker loses 2 teeth every 10 years)
Dental check-ups: 3 hours 30 minutes to 8 hours 42 minutes (2 - 5 minutes twice a year)

Illness:
Being ill: 4 years
Number of doctors: 19
Coughs & colds: 2 years 6 months
Number of aspirin/painkillers: 11,180 (215 a year)

Other:
Donating blood (48 years (ages 17 to 65) twice a year): No. of times: 96; Time spent: 6 days (1.5 hours each time); Amount of blood: 45,120 ml/45.12 litres/79.4 pints (470 ml/1 pint each time)
Complaining: Overall: 5 months; About bad service: 3 months 2 weeks (8 minutes a day)
Complaining about the weather – British: No. of times: 75,920 times (4 times a day); Time spent: 1 year 2 months 12 days (8 minutes 21 seconds a day)
Number of duvet days – Women: 8 months 15 days 12 hours (5 a year)
Optician's eye tests: 10 hours 48 minutes (25 minutes every 2 years)
Walking: 120,000 km/74,564.54 miles (24 km/14.91 miles a day)
Amount of dust inhaled: 18 kg/40 lbs

Personal Grooming & Appearance

Both Sexes:
Hair: No. of washes: 9,940 (every other day); No. of cuts: 240-500; No. of hairdressers: 4.3 (changed every 12 years); Time spent suffering bad hair: 26 years
Looking for things lost: 10 months 3 weeks (150 hours a year)
Choosing what to wear: 10 months 3 weeks (150 hours a year)
Deodorant used: 260 sticks

Showering: 2 months 9 days 12 hours or 4 months 2 weeks 5 days (5 or 10 minutes a day)

Number of umbrellas: 26 (1 every 2 years)

Men:

Getting ready for a night out: 1 month 2 weeks 5 days (a third of women's time)

Dressing – work days: 2 weeks 6 days 12 hours to 1 month 2 days 18 hours (10 to 15 minutes work days)

Pairs of underpants – American: 364 (7 pairs a year)

Pairs of socks (70 years): 2,022 pairs

Looking for missing socks: nearly 4 weeks

No longer care about appearance: 24 years (from 46 years old)

Shaving: Time spent: 7 months 2 weeks 6 days 12 hours (15 minutes work days & 25 minutes weekend); No. of shaving cuts: 260 (5 times a year)

Looking in the mirror: No. of times - 341,000; Amount of time - 6 months

Helping wife/girlfriend choose an outfit: 2 days 4 hours (1 hour a year)

Women:

Getting ready for a night out: 4 months 3 weeks 5 days 12 hours

Make-up: 6 months 2 weeks (15 minutes each morning)

Cost of bras: $5,400/£3,288.27

Lipstick used: 2.7 kg/6 lbs

Financial investment in face: $30,000/£17,900

Number of make-up styles: 5.2 (changes 10 yearly)

No longer care about appearance: 11 years (from 59 years old)

Shaving legs: 1 month 3 weeks 3 days (15 minutes twice a week)

Looking in the mirror: No. of times - 721,240 (38 times a day); Amount of time - 2 years

Dieting: Time spent: 17 years; Loss of body weight: 9 times; No. of British women who diet: 90%; All kinds of weight loss tried: 117.5 times (2.26 times a year after age 18); Time spent on New Year's diets: 8 years 8 months (2 months a year)

Relationships

Both Sexes:

Number of Romantic Partners: 14

Kissing: Calorie loss: 493,480 (26 calories a minute, 1 minute a day); Time spent: 1 week 6 days 5 minutes (1 minute a day)

Wanting a hug (70 years): 127,750 times (5 times a day)

Falling in love: up to 7 times before marrying

Sharing romantic time: 3 weeks 6 days 12 hours

Marriage: No. of times possible: 3.5 to 5.2 (10 to 15 years each); Time spent getting married: 1 hour 45 minutes to 2 hours 38 minutes (average ceremony of 30 minutes); Possible time on honeymoon: 28 days to 41 days 14 hours 24 minutes (average lasts 8 days)

Break-ups due to cheating: 4

Number of arguments – married couples: 8,320 (160 a year)

Men:

Staring at the opposite sex: about a year

Discussing their day: 2 months 5 days (5 minutes a day)

Crying: No. of times: 884 (17 times a year); Time spent: 2 days 12 hours (4 minutes a time)

Women:

Staring at the opposite sex: just over 2 months

Possibly proposing marriage: 13 times (every 4 years on Leap Year)

Discussing their day: 6 months 2 weeks (15 minutes a day)

Crying: No. of times: 3,328 (64 times a year); Time spent: 1 week 6 days 54 minutes (6 minutes a time)

Sex

Both Sexes:

Sexual partners in a lifetime: British: 10, Chinese: 19, Vietnamese: 2.5

Number of times of sex: 5,356 times (103 times a year)

Foreplay: 1 month 3 weeks 6 days 12 hours (15.5 minutes of 5,356 times of sex)

Number of times of sex in a car – Drivers: 6

Time spent on sex: 2 months 4 days 19 hours 12 minutes (30 hours a year)

Time spent on actual intercourse: 3 weeks 6 days 3 hours 36 minutes (7.3 minutes x 5,356 times)

Men:

Time spent on orgasms: 18 hours 27 minutes (12.4 seconds each)

Number of contractions: 80,340 (15 each time)
Number of thrusts during intercourse: 321,360 to 642,720 (60 to 120) and 482,040 (average 90)
Testes size increase – if they weren't to return to normal size after sex, as they do: 24,100 cm³ or 1,470.7 inches³ or 0.85 feet³ each (50% size increase of 5,356 times of sex = 2,678 of original average size)
Number of sperm ejaculated: 1,499,680,000,000 (nearly 1.5 trillion) (180 million to 400 million sperm ejaculated – averaging 280 million in each ejaculate)
Distance travelled by all sperm: 801.65 km/498.12 miles (at 43.45 km/h/27 mph and in total 18.5 hours of orgasm)
Amount of ejaculate: 14.73 litres/25.9 pints (2.75 ml/0.005 pints each of 5,356 ejaculates)
Bases of genetic information: 4,500,000,000,000,000,000,000 (4.5 sextillion) (3 billion bases on each of 1.5 trillion sperm)
Time spent removing a bra: 1 day 16 hours 5 minutes (27 seconds x 5,356 times of sex)
Thinking about sex: No. of times: 175,700,517.2 (every 7 seconds, 18 hour day - about 120 times more than women - see below).
Women:
Time spent on orgasms: 2 hours 32 minutes (1.7 seconds each)
Number of contractions: 10,712 (2 each time)
Thinking about sex: No. of times: 1,464,117.2 (every 14 minutes, 18 hour day)

Domestic & Family

Food:
Amount of food eaten: 50 tonnes/100,000 lbs
Carrot sticks eaten: 23,400 (450 a year)
Number of TV dinners eaten: 3,744 (6 a month)
Breakfast cereal: No. of bowls: 10,400 (200 a year); Amount of cereal: 306.8 kg/676 lbs (5.9 kg/13 lbs a year)
American (each): Gum: 9,880 (190 pieces a year); Milk: 5,912.4 litres/1,300 gallons (113.7 litres/25 gallons a year); Potatoes: 2,828.8 kg/6,236 lb (54.4 kg/120 lb a year); Apples: 468 kg/10,402 lb (9 kg/20 lb a year); Cheese: 707.2 kg/1,559 lb/111.4 stone (13.6 kg/29.98 lbs/2.14 stone a year); Pizza: 2,392 slices/542.36 kg/1,196 lbs (46

224

slices/10.43 kg/23 lbs a year); Ice: 2,460.6 kg/5,408 lbs (0.91 kg/2 lbs a week); M & M's: 11,113 each

French (each): Snails: 26,000 each (500 a year); Cheese: 1,268.8 kg/2,797 lb/199.8 stone (24.4 kg/53.8 lbs/3.8 stone a year)

British (each): Biscuits: 35,000; Chocolate: 494 kg/1,089 lb (9.5 kg/20.9 lb a year); Tea drunk: 94,900 cups (5 a day); Coffee drunk: 37,960 cups (2 a day)

Chocolate: Swiss: 618.8 kg/1,364 lb/93.6 stone each (11.9 kg/26.24 lbs/1.8 stone each a year), Irish: 514.8 kg/1,135 lb each (9.9 kg/21.8 lbs each a year)

Mealtimes:

Overall eating & drinking: 4 years 8 months 16 days 12 hours

Burnt home-cooked meals: 156 (3 a year, across sexes)

Lunch & dinner/tea: 8 months 2 weeks 5 days (20 minutes each); No. of times swallowing (dinner): 5,599,100 (295 times each meal); No. of dinners eaten (52 years): 18,980; Calorie loss (dinner): 949,000 (50 calories each meal)

Breakfast: Weekdays: 1 month 2 weeks 3 days (5 minutes each)/3 months 4 days (10 minutes each); Saturday or Sunday breakfast: 1 month 3 weeks 3 days (30 minutes each)

American (70 years): Eating & drinking: 3 years 7 months 3 weeks 6 days 14 hours 30 minutes; Eating 3 meals: 3 years 7 months 2 weeks 5 days 2 minutes 24 seconds (75 minutes a day for 3 meals)

French (70 years): Eating & drinking: 5 years 10 months; Eating 3 meals: 5 years 9 months 3 weeks 5 days 21 hours 7 minutes 12 seconds (2 hours a day for 3 meals)

Number of chopsticks – Chinese: 31.89 pairs each (China uses 45 billion a year & 2022 population of China is about 1.411 billion)

Time Spent in Kitchen:

Thinking about food - Men: 341,640 times (18 times a day)

Food preparation/cleaning up - Men: 8 months 2 weeks 5 days (20 minutes a day)

Looking in the fridge: just over 2 months (across sexes)

British: 2 years 7 months 6 days (8 hours a week), including 8 months 2 weeks 4 days relaxing there

Italian: Preparing meals: 8 months 2 weeks 5 days (20 minutes a day); Watching cookery programmes: 1 year 2 months 3 weeks 5 days 12

hours (4 hours a week); Cooking: 9 months 7 days 12 hours (20 minutes a day)

Children:

Diapers/nappies: 3,500 each child

Questions – Mother: (for 6 years each child - 4 to 10 years) 630,720 questions from each child (105,120 questions a year)

PTA meetings: (for 13 years each child - 5 to 18 years) 19 hours 30 minutes (1.5 hours meeting,1 a year) or 9 days 18 hours (1.5 hours meeting, 1 a month)

Parents reading to child: (up to 10 years old) 1 month 2 weeks 6 days 12 hours (140 minutes a week)

Pets:

Number of pets: 24

Number of cats: 3.6 (average cat lifespan - 15 years & UK legal age for cat-ownership - 16 years, so possible 54 years of owning one cat at a time to 70 years old)

Number of dogs: 5.4 (average dog lifespan of 10 years and UK legal age of dog ownership is 16 years – so possible 54 years of owning one dog at a time)

Walking the dog: 3 weeks 4 days 4 hours 48 minutes (1 hour a week of one 10 year dog lifespan at a time)

Housework:

Overall (including cooking, gardening, cleaning, laundry): 6 years 10 months 3 weeks 3 days (22.5 hours a week) – *including* …

Laundry: No. of loads per household: 18,200 (350 a year); Amount of time: 2 years 7 months 3 weeks 3 days

Washing machines bought: 7

Making the bed: Distance walked – across sexes: 332.8 km/208 miles (6.4 km/4 miles a year), Women - 259.6 km/162.24 miles (78% of time)

Running a dishwasher: 10,400 times (200 times a year)

Woman picking up man's clothes: 2 days

Other.

Number of mattresses: 5.2 (10 year lifespan)

Number of pillows: 34.7 (18 month lifespan)

Number of toilets: 1 (50 year lifespan)

Number of vacuum cleaners: 5.2 (10 year lifespan)

Money & Shopping

Money:

Time getting cash (bank & ATM): 11 days 22 hours 5 minutes (5.5 hours a year)

Number of new coins – America: 1.7 to 2 sets of each coin (25 to 30 year lifespan of American coins)

Number of coupons seen: 162,240 (60 a week)

Shopping:

General: No. of times: 15,652 (301 times a year); Time spent: 2 years 4 months 1 week 6 days (399 hours 46 minutes a year) – *including* …

Food shopping: No. of times: 4,368 (84 times a year); Time spent: 7 months 6 days (94 hours 55 minutes a year)

Gift shopping: No. of times: 988 (19 times a year); Time spent: 2 months 2 weeks 5 days (36 hours 17 minutes a year)

Window shopping: No. of times: 2,652 (51 times a year); Time spent: 3 months 2 weeks 12 hours (48 hours 51 minutes a year)

Clothes shopping: No. of times: 1,560 (30 times a year); Time spent: 7 months 6 days (100 hours 48 minutes a year)

Shoe shopping: No. of times: 780 (15 times a year); Time spent: 2 months 3 weeks 5 days 12 hours (40 hours 30 minutes a year)

Accessories (handbags, scarves, jewellery, etc): No. of times: 936 (18 times a year); Time spent: 2 months 5 days (29 hours 31 minutes a year)

Toiletries: No. of times: 1,404 (27 times a year); Time spent: 1 month 6 days (17 hours 33 minutes a year)

Books: No. of times: 2,964 (57 times a year); Time spent: 2 months 1 week 1 day 12 hours (31 hours 21 minutes a year)

Supermarket: Queuing: 1 month 3 weeks 3 days 36 minutes (29 minutes a week); Collecting up belongings at supermarket checkout: 3 hours 51 minutes (3.17 seconds x 4,368 times in 52 years – see 'Food Shopping' above)

Leisure

General:

Recreation - socialising, exercising, watching TV: Women - 11 years 3 months 7 days (5.2 hours a day), Men - 13 years (6 hours a day) *including* …

Socializing: 1 year 7 months 2 weeks (45 minutes a day)
People:
Friends – Men: 396
People we meet: 8,747,485.6 (124,964.08 a year)
Shaking hands: Men: 16,224 times (6 times a week), Women: 8,112 times (3 times a week)
Telling lies: Men: 56,940 times (3 times a day), Women: 37,960 times (2 times a day)
Apologising: 13,520 times (5 times a week)
Number of times of new friends: 7.4 (50% replaced 7 yearly)
Phone calls to mother: Women: No. of calls: 18,980 (1 a day); Time spent: 9 months (21 minutes a day),
Drinks:
Amount of beer – British: 3,796 litres/6,680 pints/835 gallons (73 litres/128 pints each a year)
Amount of beer – Czech: 8,112 litres/14,272 pints/1,784 gallons (156 litres/274.4 pints each a year)
Wine bought – American: 520 bottles (10 bottles per household a year)
Television:
Watching television (70 years): 9 years 8 months 15 days
Number of TV commercials seen: 1,599,999.96 (52 years) or 2,153,846.10 (70 years) (30,769.23 a year)
Number of 30-second TV commercials: 1,040,000 (52 years) or 1,400,000 (70 years) (20,000 a year)
Watching or hearing commercial ads: 2 years 11 months 3 days (52 years) or 3 years 1 month 1 week 1 day 9 hours 36 minutes (70 years) (81 minutes a day)
Lies seen in soap operas: 83,824 (6.2 lies in an hour of soap opera, 1 hour a day, 5 days a week)
Number of American soap characters put into comas: 332.8 (64 every 10 years)
Television cereal ads – American: 67.6 million (52 years) or 91 million (70 years) (1.3 million a year)
Other:
Number of Olympic Games: 26 (summer and winter alternate 2-yearly)
Breaking the law (speeding, parking, etc): 1,196 times (23 times a year)

Church services: 3 weeks 5 days (1 hour once a month)
Reading: 1 year 1 month 2 days 12 hours (30 minutes a day)
Watching football: 1 month 3 days 12 hours
Sunbathing: 3 months 6 days 12 hours
Number of chances to vote: British: 10.4 (5-yearly General Elections), American: 13 (4-yearly Presidential Elections)
Number of US Censuses (70 years): 7 (every 10 years)

Technology

Fixing electronic glitches: 2 months 5 days (5 minutes a day)
Computers:
Logging on: 9 months 2 weeks 4 days (11.3 hours a month)
Number of passwords: 260 to 312 (5 or 6 changes a year)
Time waiting for downloads: 3 months 4 weeks 1 day (9 minutes a day)
Time on the Internet: 7 years 4 month 3 weeks 6 days 12 hours (24 hours a week)
Time on social networking: 5 years 4 months 3 weeks 2 days 22 hours 33 minutes 36 seconds (2.5 hours a day)
Playing on-line games: 1 year 2 months 3 weeks 5 days 12 hours (4 hours a week)
Wikipedia: Odds of any daily visit: 103% (4.95 billion internet users/5.1 billion Wiki users); No. of pages per visit: 3; Time per visit: 3.54 minutes
Phones:
Cell phones: No. of times checking: Millennials - 2,847,000 (150 times a day), Average person –1,100,840 (58 times a day); No. of texts sent/received: 664,300 (35 a day); Time spent writing texts: 5 months 2 weeks 4 days (45 seconds each)
Phones: Time used: 7 years 2 months 12 days (3 hours 15 minutes a day); Time on hold at call centres: 4 months 1 week 2 days 12 hours (60 hours a year); Number of calls made/received: 94,640 (5 a day)

Travel

Overall travelling: 6 years
Cars:
Number of cars owned: 9 (first 2 before 24 years old)

Cleaning: Automatic car wash: 1 week 6 days 8 minutes 30 seconds (7 minutes once a week); Inside: 1,248 times (twice a month); Cleaning out glovebox: 26 times (2 yearly)

Traffic: Queueing: 3 months 3 weeks 1 day 12 hours (1 hour a week)

Waiting at traffic lights: 6 months (minimum 30 seconds for a red light)

Honking car horn: 15,250 times

Swearing as a car driver: 32,000 times

Accidents: Claims: 2.91 times (every 17.9 years average); No. of accidents: 3 to 4

Driving when lost: Miles wasted - Men: 23,097.36 km/14,352 miles (444.18 km/276 miles a year), Women: 21,423.48 km/13,312 miles (411.99 km/256 miles a year); Petrol wasted – Men: £2,000/$3,300

Number of times a driver is locked out of their car: 5

Parking the car - Women: 12 days

Other:

Aircraft travel: 2 months 5 days (average 2.5 hours a month)

Waiting for trains: 3 weeks 6 days 5 hours 30 minutes

Distance travelled in space (70 years): 65,822,877,711.36 km/40,900,440,000 miles (Earth travels through space at 107,343.25 km/h/66,700 mph and 2,576,237.88 km/1,600,800 miles in 24 hours)

Number of times round the sun (70 years): 70 (Earth takes 1 year to go round the sun once); Distance travelled: 66,118,932,633.6 km/ 41,084,400,000 miles (speed of orbit - 107,800 km/h/67,000 mph)

Number of spins on the Earth (70 years): 25,500 (Earth rotates 365 times a year); Miles travelled: 986,849,740.8 km/613,200,000 miles (the Earth spins at 1,609.34 km/h/1,000 mph at the Equator)

Work

Number of jobs: 10.4 (18 to 70 years as retirement age) (new job every 5 years)

Work: 11 years 5 months 4 days 12 hours in working lifetime (8 hours x 5 days a week is 11 weeks 3 days a year)

Late for work: 190 times

Off sick: 1 year 1 day

Wasting working day: 7 months (1.7 hours a day of 11.43 working years)

Work coffee breaks: 1 month 1 day (15 minutes each working day)

Time dealing with spam & unwanted calls and emails: 1 month 3 weeks 6 days 12 hours (29 minutes each working day)

Use of backspace & delete keys – Office Workers: 356,616 times (600 times a week, 11.43 working years)

On work phone: 4 years (excluding working from home)

Time on work emails: 3 years 11 months 5 days 9 hours 36 minutes (650 hours a year x 11.43 years)

Mouse clicks in working day: 3 months 4 days (427.2 clicks a day, 1 second each)

Ciggie breaks: 3 months (a 5 minute break x 11.43 working years)

Diary Days

Celebrating own birthday: 2 months 12 days (24 hours each, 70 years); Leap Year birthdays – 29th February: 2 weeks 3 days 12 hours (every 4 years)

Woman's birthday promises of life changes: 52 times

Birthday – American: No. of cards: 350 (5 a year); No. of gifts: 280 (4 a year)

Number of 'Friday the 13th's (70 years): 140 to 210 (2 to 3 a year)

Number of solar eclipses: 104 (52 years) and 140 (70 years) (at least 2 solar eclipses a year by a new moon)

Number of solar cycles lived through: 4.7 (52 years) and 6.4 (70 years) (11 years each cycle)

Blue Moons seen: 18.9 (about every 33 months)

Miscellaneous

Using vending machines: 5,980 times (115 times a year)

Spiders (70 years): No. in a house: 11,010,550 (estimated 32,750 spiders in a house, each with average lifespan across sexes of 76 days and assuming replaced with 1 offspring 336.2 times); No. of bugs eaten: 22,021,100,000 (each spider eats 2,000 bugs a year)

Number of Post Office trips: 780 (15 times a year)

Number of new crop patterns: 13,000 (250 a year)

Checking horoscopes – Women: 8,112 times (3 times a week)

Sorting junk mail: 5 months 5 days (3 days a year)

Extra time of life (70 years): 0.00051 seconds (each day lengthens 0.00000002 seconds)

Time After Time

Habits

"Not this week. I'm
washing my hair."

Time After Time
Habits

It takes an average of 66 days to form a habit or break a habit. In this chapter, these are the average habits of a normal person – some do them more; some do them less. You don't have OCD if you do these things more than the average person. If a habit doesn't bother you or anybody else and you don't overvalue how important it is - it's a habit and not an obsession. But ... if you want to spend time more profitably on other things, you may choose to change a habit.

NO TIES! I'M FREE! IT'S WONDERFUL!

* ❖ "We are what we repeatedly do." *Aristotle*
* ❖ "The definition of insanity is doing the same thing over and over and expecting different results." *Albert Einstein*
* ❖ "What you are is what you have been. What you'll be is what you do now." *Buddha*

Habits: Both Sexes

Your Body
Laugh 17 times a day
Apologize 5 times a week
Second-guess ourselves 10 times a day
Talk to ourselves 6 times a day
Get frightened twice a week
Sneeze or blow our nose 250 times a year
Forget 80% of what we learn in a day
Yawn 5 times a day

Stay awake for 7 minutes before falling asleep
Touch our face 2,000 to 3,000 times a day

Health & Wellbeing
Take 215 aspirin or pain relief a year
Wash our hands 12 times a day
British: Complain about the weather 4 times a day
Break the law 23 times a year

Personal Grooming & Appearance
Tie our shoes 3 times a day
Keep the same hairdresser for 12 years
Change our mind about what to wear 3 times in the morning

Relationships
Are in a relationship for 2 years 9 months
Want a hug 5 times a day
American: Receive 5 birthday cards and 4 birthday presents
Married couple: Argue 160 times a year in bed – 3 times a week

Sex
Have sex 103 times a year (just under twice a week)

Domestic & Family
Burn 3 home-cooked meals a year
Clean the inside of the car twice a month
Clean the car glovebox every 2 years
Clean the fridge every 3.5 months (110 days) – 3 times a year
American: In a year, have: 50 pizzas, 72 TV dinners, 156 desserts
& 70 hot dogs
Open our home fridge door 22 times a day
Use a favourite coffee mug 2,100 times before replacing it
Go to Starbucks 6 times a month
Nearly always sit in the same place when eating at home
Dread making dinner on a Saturday and a Monday
Have a 5 to 10 minute breakfast on a work day
Have a 30 minute breakfast on the weekend

Like to eat breakfast in front of the TV
Spend 20 minutes on lunch and dinner/tea
American: spend 25 minutes on a meal
French: spend 40 minutes on a meal
Send 20 Christmas cards

Money & Shopping
Use an ATM 80 times a year
Spend 45 minutes on a grocery shopping trip
Ignore 99.3% of the items in the grocery store in a year
Throw away about half our junk mail without reading it

Leisure
Spend 45 minutes a day socializing
Have 3 pictures taken a month
Read for 30 minutes a day
Read the front page of the Sunday papers first, then coupon inserts
Spend 9 minutes playing with our children on Christmas morning
Buy 4 DVD's a year
See 6.2 lies in an hour of a soap opera
American: Go to the movies 4.3 times a year

Technology
Check the time 100 times a day
Make 1,825 phone calls a year
Spend 5 minutes a day fixing electronic glitches
Computer Users
Check Wikipedia 3 times and for a total of 10.62 minutes a day
Change our password 5 or 6 times a year
Open emails up to 48 hours after they're sent
Spend 2.5 hours a day on social networks – 17.5 hours a week,
including 7 hours – Facebook, over 4.5 hours – YouTube
Spend 8 hours a week checking emails
Smartphone Users
Touch our smartphones 2,617 times
Buy a new cell phone every 2 years
Send/Receive 35 texts a day

235

Open a text message 4 minutes after it's been sent
Have an average of 200 contacts on our cell phone
Spend 55 minutes a day texting

Work (Office Workers)
Use 9 to 10 sticky notes a day
Clean out the staff fridge twice a year
Spend 13 hours of the working week dealing with emails
Lose 970 calories, click the mouse 700 times, and move it
35.27m/38.57 yards/0.08 miles in a week dealing with emails
Take 15 minutes for a coffee break
Spend 29 minutes of an 8-hour working day dealing with spam, and
unwanted emails and calls

Habits: Women

Personal Grooming & Appearance
Diet 4 times a year
Have an 'I hate my body moment' at least once a day
Start planning a Saturday night outfit from 1.35 pm on the Wednesday
Think about fashion 91 times a day
Think about their hair 40 times a day
Change their hair style 4 times a year (18 to 35 year olds)
Spend 172 hours a year putting on make-up (3 hours 19 mins a week)
Change their make-up style each decade
Spend 15 minutes putting on make-up in the morning
Use a lipstick 293 times before it's finished
Check themselves in a mirror 38 times in the day

Relationships
Are 30.8 years old on their wedding day
Spend 15 minutes telling their partner how their day was
Cry for 6 minutes at a time, 64 times a year
Lie the most about their looks in their online dating profiles
Think about calling their Mum 5 times a day
Call their mother at least once a day

Shake hands 3 times a week
Lie twice a day
Tell a secret after 32 minutes

Sex
Prefer sex in the dark
Shut their eyes when they kiss
Think about sex once every 14 minutes

Domestic & Family
Answer over 105,000 questions from their child in a year
Italians: Spend 20 minutes a day preparing food
Italians: Spend 4 hours a week watching TV cookery programmes
British: Spend 8 hours a week in the kitchen, including 20 minutes a
day relaxing there

Money & Shopping
Think about grocery shopping 5 times a day
Dislike doing grocery shopping on a Monday
Buy 1.5 bottles of wine a month

Leisure
Spend 5 hours a day on leisure, including 4.5 hours a week
watching TV

Miscellaneous
Have up to 5 duvet days a year
Waste 411.99 km/256 miles a year driving while lost and
not asking for directions
Check their horoscope 3 times a week

Habits: Men

Personal Grooming & Appearance
Take 15 minutes to shave on work days & 25 minutes on the weekend
Take 10 to 15 minutes to get dressed on a work day

237

Check if their zipper is down 3 times a day
Check themselves in a mirror 19 times in the day

Relationships
Lie the most about how much money they make in their
online dating profiles
Say 'I love you' 1.2 times a day
Are 32.7 years old on their wedding day
Take under 5 minutes to tell their partner how their day was
Cry for 4 minutes at a time, and for 17 times a year
Think about calling their Mum every other day, and 1 in 3 call
at least once a week
Shake hands 6 times a week
Lie three times a day
Think about smiling 10 times a day

Sex
Think about sex every 7 seconds
Thrust 60 to 120 times during intercourse

Money & Shopping
Think about grocery shopping once every other day
Dislike doing grocery shopping on a Thursday
Buy 1 bottle of wine a month

Leisure
Take 14 alcoholic drinks a week – marathon runners
Spend 6 hours a day on leisure activities, including 2 hours on
sports/exercise

Miscellaneous
Waste 444.18 km/276 miles a year driving while lost and
not asking for directions
Are four times more likely than women to sleep naked
Think about food 18 times a day
Spend 20 minutes a day preparing food and drinks and cleaning the
kitchen

Time Springs Eternal

Survival Odds

"A bee stung him and he accidentally
kicked a dog that chased him
into the road. Luckily he got hit
by an ambulance."

Time Springs Eternal
Survival Odds

They say the only two things you can be sure of in life are taxes and death. But what's the chance of dying from other than old age?

These are the odds in our battle for survival.

20 trillion to 1	being killed by a meteoroid
5 billion to 1	being killed by space debris
734,400,000 to 1	being killed by hail
500,000,000 to 1	being killed on a 5-mile bus trip
300,000,000 to 1	being killed in a fairground accident
300,000,000 to 1	dying on a roller coaster
300,000,000 to 1	dying from measles
250,000,000 to 1	being killed by a falling coconut
112,000,000 to 1	being killed by a vending machine
32,000,000 to 1	dying from a mountain lion attack in California
30,589,556 to 1	dying from nightwear igniting or melting
20,000,000 to 1	being killed in a terrorist attack
11,000,000 to 1	dying in a plane crash
10,440,000 to 1	dying in an elevator
10,000,000 to 1	dying from parts falling from an airplane
10,000,000 to 1	being killed by the escape of radiation from a nearby nuclear power station
10,000,000 to 1	dying from a tornado
5,005,564 to 1	dying from contact with hot tap water
4,400,000 to 1	left-handers being killed using a right-handed product
4,235,477 to 1	dying from being bitten or struck by mammals (other than dogs or humans)

3,700,000 to 1	being killed by a shark
3,500,000 to 1	being killed by a snake
3,441,325 to 1	dying from legal execution
3,441,325 to 1	dying from contact with a venomous animal or plant
3,000,000 to 1	dying from food poisoning
3,000,000 to 1	being killed by freezing
2,300,000 to 1	dying from falling off a ladder
2,320,000 to 1	being killed by lightning
2,100,000 to 1	being_killed by a bear in Yellowstone National Park
2,000,000 to 1	dying by falling out of bed
1,428,377 to 1	dying from overexertion, travel or privation
1,000,000 to 1	dying from flesh-eating bacteria
840,000 to 1	dying in the bath tub
615,488 to 1	dying in a fireworks accident
500,000 to 1	being killed in a train crash
500,000 to 1	being killed by a tsunami
500,000 to 1	being killed by an asteroid colliding with Earth in the next 100 years
370,035 to 1	dying from choking on food
225,107 to 1	dying from exposure to heat, cold, earthquake or flood
144,899 to 1	dying from being bitten by a dog or colliding with it
131,890 to 1	dying from an earthquake
107,787 to 1	dying in an explosion
100,000 to 1	dying from skydiving
86,000 to 1	being killed by poisoning
81,524 to 1	dying from exposure to smoke, fire, and flames
79,842 to 1	dying from contact with hornets, wasps, and bees
68,388 to 1	dying in a severe storm

241

43,500 to 1	being killed in an accident at work
18,690 to 1	being murdered
16,421 to 1	dying from an assault
9,380 to 1	dying from intentional self-harm
8,942 to 1	dying from accidental drowning
8,200 to 1	women drivers – being killed on Friday the 13th
8,000 to 1	being killed in a road accident
5,000 to 1	dying from electrocution
5,000 to 1	being killed in a car crash
4,472 to 1	dying on a bicycle
1,820 to 1	dying from any kind of injury during the next year
218 to 1	dying from a fall
77 to 1	being killed in any sort of transportation accident
69 to 1	being killed in any sort of non-transportation accident
63 to 1	dying from flu
15 to 1	dying climbing Mount Everest
5 to 1	dying from a cancer
3 to 1	dying from heart disease
2.5 to 1	dying from a heart attack or a stroke

In Bude, Cornwall, England, the End of the World Society decided it was time we all said 'goodbye' at a Doomsday Party. But they had to cancel the big bash when they were refused a special late-night drinks licence. The local magistrates said the end of the world wasn't a special event.

Time for a Change
Sickie Excuses

"As we're both taking a sickie, I'll plan our holiday while you do the cooking, dishes, shopping, laundry, mow the lawn, clean the car ... "

Time for a Change
Sickie Excuses

If anything in this book inspires you to fulfil as-yet-unfulfilled ambitions, and you need time by pulling a sickie, try these excuses. You can decide the chances of your boss buying your story.

> 5% of us take a day off work because we stubbed our toe.
> 53% of us think the best excuse to get some time off work is problems with our home (eg plumbing, AC, boiler problems).
> But, for those of us genuinely sick, 1.14 billion prescriptions were dispensed in England and 4.76 billion in America (2022).

You're afraid that you're possessed by Satan and you don't want to put your work colleagues at risk.
Odds of being considered possessed by Satan:
7,000 to 1. They're stacked against you, but this should get you several months – or even years - off work and a room in a comfortable big house with kindly people wearing white, and you won't even have to do your own laundry.

You have Ergophobia ...
... which is the fear of work. You could have weeks, or even months, off. But you need to convince your doctor of your problem and, chances are, you'll be referred for counselling.
But, hey – that could be useful for other things instead, like quitting smoking, your fear of vampires, your irresistible attraction to shoes ...

Your tarantula needs re-training.
The odds of contact with venomous spiders are 1 in 379,841. Your tarantula had an off-day and bit you. Could be a few days off work, and a heavy dose of precautionary antibiotics – and then you could be suffering the side-effects of those. All in all, you could spend a happy week stroking your tarantula back to its normal cheerful self. After all, it was probably just missing your company.

You think you've got a cold coming so you need to stay home and have sex.
A medical study in Pennsylvania found that people who have sex once or twice a week have their immune systems boosted slightly. So, being a responsible employee, and to avoid the possibility of spreading a cold round at work, you need to stay home and boost your immune system with sex. Could take a couple of days. Your boss is likely to agree to this excuse. He or she will want to use it themselves at some future date.

You've decided to serve your country as an astronaut.
From the Greek, meaning 'Space Sailor', chances are 13.2 million to 1 against you doing it. Basic requirements to be an American astronaut are: be a US Citizen, get a Bachelor's degree in a science and then 3 years' experience, 1,000 hours or more in command as a jet pilot, pass the NASA space physical and psychological test, be a team player and then train for several years to go into space. But you might pull it off as a sickie excuse if your boss is a Star Wars fan. And, working from stage 1 of not having any degree, you could try for 10 years or more off work. Your boss needs to keep your job open just in case you have to remain earth-bound. But it's the least she or he can do when you're trying for a 'giant leap for mankind'.

You injured yourself using a chain saw to clean the BBQ.
Odds: 4,464 to 1 for injury from a chain saw, but worth a try for at least one day off, especially after a public holiday.

You found a four-leaf clover, so you need the day to do all the lotteries and chance games you can find.
Finding a four-leaf clover on the first try: odds of 10,000 to 1. Your boss may suddenly become your best friend, and give you the day off with great encouragement to invest a few pounds or dollars for him or her too.

You tripped over your goldfish.
Annually, just under 100,000 Americans go to the Emergency Room because of a tripping accident from a pet in their house. Explain that you tripped carrying Nemo's goldfish bowl to the kitchen to be cleaned and narrowly avoided squashing him under your size 10's. But in the process, the said size 10's met the water, and you elegantly slid towards the sofa where your ankle stuck firmly between it and the floor. When the paramedics arrived, you begged them to first save your loyal and faithful Nemo before they treated your ankle sprain. Should get you a few days off and sympathy from every female member of staff for your thoughtfulness towards Nemo.

You can't sleep because you're worried that an asteroid will hit the Earth.
The chance that Earth will experience a catastrophic collision with an asteroid in the next 100 years: 1 in 5,000. Tell your boss that – however much she or he says the odds are against it happening - the only way you'll come out of your nice safe house is if she or he will explain the astrophysics to you to disprove your fear – with PowerPoint diagrams. Should take at least a couple of weeks for your boss to do that while you're cosied in at home.

You've been asked to run for President.

Your odds of becoming a US president: 10,000,000 to 1. You must be a US Citizen, have lived in the US for at least 14 years and be 35 years or over. If you qualify, you could get 4 years off work to prepare for an election. Give your boss a formal-looking letter from the White House. Yep. He or she will believe you - especially based on the excellent standard of your work. Good luck with that one.

You're being audited by the IRS.

Odds: 175 to 1. A good chance that your boss might believe this – and can she or he prove it's not true? So go for at least 2 days off to get your paperwork into order – and you'll probably get an extra day or two, in sympathy, from your boss. Heck – try for the whole week.

You speared your nose with a toothpick.

About 8,800 people a year are injured using toothpicks. You could describe, in great detail, your embarrassment of when your arm slipped on the edge of the dinner table and you speared your nose instead of picking your teeth. And, as you were next to the Lady Mayoress, you accidentally shouldered her in the process, sending her coffee flying over the central table flower display. Most important is to emphasise this high social connection by which your boss will want to befriend you and it should guarantee you a day or two off to nurse your nosebleed.

A psychic said you'd win an Academy Award.

Odds of winning one: 11,500 to 1. Odds of becoming a Movie Star: 1 in 1,505,000. Trouble is - you've never done any acting. But you'll always regret it if you don't at least try - for the sake of the company that you can thank in your Oscar acceptance speech. Will they sponsor you? Your boss will undoubtedly say no, so follow up with … you'll need at least 3 years to train for your debut acting role and then to gain enough experience to win that coveted Oscar. So if he or she would give you at least 5 years off work – you'll happily help at the works pantomime each year for free, to show your gratitude.

You can't work because you're officially dead.

Considering the number of people in the USA, the odds of being wrongly declared dead by a Social Security data entry mistake are quite high - 1 in 23,483 - and in your favour. And you have to prove you are, in fact, very much an alive 'you'. So, what boss can deny you days off work, or even weeks, and maybe months – as could happen if your paperwork gets held up or you take a while to complete the necessary forms and maybe accidentally send them to the wrong address?

You're being interviewed by a tabloid about seeing a UFO last Tuesday evening when you fell out of the pub.

Odds of spotting a UFO today: 3,000,000 to 1. Weren't you lucky to see it?! A day off, easily, and when the 'exposé' is published - a free copy of the magazine for your boss.

They wouldn't want you back at work without your normal level of grasp.

After a three-week holiday, your IQ can drop by as much as 20%. You can assure your boss that you'll work on getting it back up to the level he or she expects of you, at home – doing mind puzzles (TV game shows), memory games (the round of drinks), and mathematical puzzles (adding up your golf and darts scores). Alternatively, if you can't swing a few days off, you could do a four-day week and claim your brain can't cope with the other day. All in all – a good bet as a sickie excuse and it's based on scientific fact.

248

Your earring hit you in the eye.
An average of 55,700 people are injured by jewellery each year. Frantic disco dancing and long dangly earrings don't go well in the same place and time. Other than your swollen eye, you might want to add that you tripped over your handbag strap trying to get a mirror, and banged your head on the table. Should be at least a couple of days off – or until you think your hangover's gone.

You need to check if your armadillo can swim.
This gets you a full 24 hours off. And maybe another day, if your armadillo doesn't fancy the tepid bath water that day. Armadillos get an average of 18.5 hours of sleep a day. But they also like to swim. So, with your armadillo being asleep for three quarters of the day, you need a clear 24 hours to be with it, waiting for it to have its happy splash around in your bath.

You got a royal flush in poker on the first five cards dealt.
The odds are: 649,740 to 1. With your colossal winnings (having put a bet on yourself at the local betting shop), the begging letters are depressing you and you need a day or two off work to cope with them. You can stop writing the letters in a couple of days - you don't need to, now that you're rich.

Your peanut butter became a national security risk.
Not sure of the odds, but jars of peanut butter are the items most often mistaken for explosives by airport scanners. So – fair to middling on the scale of feasible sickie excuses. It's best if you go into some detail to sound authentic: 'I was flying back from seeing my sick aunt who knows how much I love the stuff and, with her last few cents, she bought me a jar of peanut butter, bless her. And the

airport scanner picked up what they said was an explosive in my luggage. I was spread-eagle surrounded by armed guards when they found it was my jar of PB. It took a while to sort it all out, and I'll need a few days to recover and answer all the calls from my aunt. She's very worried, you know. I tried to calm her down, talking about the weather and my barometer. But, after the airport incident, she thought I said beretta and thinks I'm on the Most Wanted List'.

A meteor landed on your house and you've got to repair the roof.

Odds of a meteor landing on your house: 82,138,880,000,000 to 1. It really did happen.
True story, you say. And luckily it was only your house in the whole neighbourhood. But the problem isn't the meteor. It's getting a builder to come out today. They're always in high demand, so your boss should believe that, and have to give you at least a week off cos you have to call the builder every day to see if he's free.

You've written a best-seller, and have a book promotion tour.

Odds of writing a New York Times best seller:
1 in 220. Mention that the book includes a very understanding boss and that your literary agent said not to give up your day job. Should get you at least a month off with your job held open. Downside – you should give a copy of the book to your boss. But you could give them a taster, instead, and hope they'll forget about the book. Try this: 'A tale of Religion, Sex, Mystery and Royalty … "*My God. I'm pregnant. Who dunnit? said the Duchess*"'.

Time Index

"How much time
do you want?"

Time Index

Here, you can pick a time frame for your own activity, and see what's happening around you and around the world, as depicted in this book, for that amount of time.

253

Reach for the Stars

Acknowledgement

With many thanks to the websites of the free and public domain clipart and illustrations that have been an important part of this book, and to the very talented people who contribute to those websites of:

https://freesvg.org

https://openclipart.org

https://pixabay.com

https://www.wpclipart.com

https://www.pdclipart.org

https://thegraphicsfairy.com

https://www.clipartden.com

https://www.free-graphics.com

Printed in Great Britain
by Amazon